LISTENING!

LISTENING!

Jeffrey Hugh Newman

Walnut Road Press

Published in the United States by
Walnut Road Press LLC
One Riverfront Plaza, 11th Floor
Newark, New Jersey 07102

ISBN: 978-0615922027

10 9 8 7 6 5 4 3 2 1

IN MEMORIAM

To my beloved son,

Jon,

to whom this book is dedicated.

May the world overflow with young men like Jon who was a great son to me and his mother, a great husband to Angella and a great father to Aviva and Ayla.

Jon's kindness, love, warmth, and maturity beyond his years is a source of inspiration to all who knew him.

Perhaps the true measure of anyone's time on this Earth is how others perceived him. Jon was considered by each and every one of his friends as their single best friend – a true hallmark of a life well spent and beautifully lived.

He was my best friend, too.

ACKNOWLEDGMENTS

The first acknowledgement belongs to the Creator ... my books have been "in me" for years, but He allowed me the pleasure and fulfillment of sharing it with others. This has given me the opportunity to make an impression on the lives of others, howsoever insignificant. To allow me to feel that I am somehow giving back ... I will always be grateful.

I thank the many people who have made an imprint on my life. I have been blessed. My first wife, Linda, who is one of the kindest people I know. My second wife, Sheryl, who died from cancer. She was one of the most graceful persons I have yet to know. She brought out the best in everyone she touched.

My parents, Mark and Gloria, my brother, Mark, and my children, Alyssa and Jon, each of whom, in entirely different ways, have had varying positive impacts on my growth and development.

Michael Kercheval and his incredible staff at the International Council of Shopping Centers, all of whom trusted me, and trust me to participate as a speaker at many of their events and as a leader of several committees.

Patricia Karetsky, who catalyzed me to start writing by advising it only requires an hour a day, and Ron Pompei, who constantly assured me that I had something worthwhile to communicate.

Victoria Wright, who constantly challenged me to write better, make my work clearer, make it "sing."

All of my friends and colleagues, who, in a variety of everyday little ways, helped me to grow, learn to laugh with myself, accept myself and appreciate myself.

Steven Gross, Chairman of my law firm, who has been both a friend and mentor, not just to me, but to all of my partners. Max Crane, Managing Partner of my law firm, for his continuing support of my efforts in creating my books. Both true leaders.

I am especially thankful to all of my muses. How lucky and grateful am I to have multiple muses. My fiancée, Barbara. My colleague, Marcia, my colleague, Patrick, who created the graphic designs, my terrific former assistant, Celeste, and my terrific current assistant, Carolyn.

Special thanks to my super motivators … my grandchildren, Lia, Ari, Aviva, Eli, and Ayla.

Lastly, to all those who have come before me with self-help and other motivational works. I seek not to stand on their shoulders; rather, to someday perhaps stand shoulder-to-shoulder.

Table *of* Contents

Chapter 1

THE SKILL OF HEARING

When I was in first grade at P.S. 114, I just wanted to be the teacher's pet. Mrs. Capely was pretty and smart. She always dressed nicely. I thought she was a goddess. Perhaps she wasn't, but in my adoring eyes, she more than qualified. I had lots of fun and good experiences in first grade, but I will always remember the afternoon when our class had, for the first time, music appreciation.

It was a surprise, completely out of sync with our routine. Was recess cancelled? Was that a record player on her desk? I couldn't quite see it from my little seat. Mrs. Capely asked us to sit still. Then, she carefully pulled a record from its sleeve, placed it on the turntable, and set the needle. Although I didn't know at the time, we heard the beginning of Beethoven's 5th Symphony.

After a while—it was probably only five minutes, but it seemed like an eternity to me—Mrs. Capely stopped the music. Silence fell over the class. Had someone been talking or fidgeting or worse? Mrs. Capely turned and pointed to Marlene, seated at the desk directly across from my row. I hadn't ever really noticed Marlene before. I barely knew who she was. At that stage in my life, girls warranted scant, if any, notice. The entire class stared at Marlene. What had she done wrong? We eagerly awaited the scolding.

What Mrs. Capely said would resonate within me for the rest of my life.

"Look at Marlene," said our teacher with a smile. "She has been listening. She has been really appreciating the music. She closed her eyes while I was playing the music. Marlene really knows how to listen to and appreciate the music. Good for you, Marlene. Now class, try listening the way Marlene does."

I couldn't believe it! Marlene was the teacher's pet. Mrs. Capely was praising Marlene for what I thought was her napping. Yet, that is what happened. Of course, wanting the same approval from Mrs. Capely, I decided to do the exact same thing. So, when Mrs. Capely restarted the music, I closed my eyes. I vaguely remember liking it better with my eyes closed. It was as if I could hear—and even see—more with my eyes closed.

I was never to be the object of Mrs. Capely's special positive attention. Yet, her music appreciation lesson has remained with me. It eventually translated into hearing better, absorbing what I hear better, whether the music is from a recording or right from someone's vocal chords! I learned to listen better.

The lesson I learned was a lesson for a lifetime.

If you want to be more effective as a negotiator, counselor, doctor, lawyer, boss, colleague, parent, lover, friend, you must master the art of listening. You must appreciate it and realize its power.

Remember grade school? How often were you admonished for not listening? How many times did someone say:

- Listen!

- Be quiet and listen!

- Stop fidgeting and listen!

- Sit down and listen!

- Pay attention!

Listening is an acquired skill, a critical tool for general learning. We are asked to listen, told to listen, warned to listen, threatened if we don't listen. Listening is a crucial and fundamental skill, yet we are not taught to listen. Listening is difficult and under-appreciated, and no one teaches us how to do it.

LISTENING!

The obstacles to acquiring good listening skills are many. Most of us cannot avoid the sweet calls—the distractions—that beckon us into the trap of poor listening. Most of us, if we were to be graded in listening, would flunk.

You may be thinking, "Hey, not me!" You think you're a good listener, because:

- You graduated from high school, college, etc.

- You earned good grades.

- You would have goofed up many more things (you did!).

- You would have had many more detentions.

- You would have had much less fun.

You just proved that you could hear. Your skills were good enough to get you through. So, what's missing? There is a critical difference between listening and hearing; the gap between them must be bridged. A good analogy is cooking. Anyone can fry an egg. And with a cookbook recipe, we can prepare a meal by rote. But, by going the next step or two—by investing our thought and focus and recognizing the egg as one element in our culinary production, we can add to it the cream, the onion, the pepper, the cheese, and the spices to create an "omelettic masterpiece."

Even good hearing takes effort. Don't believe me? Remember the last time you were late—and lost? You asked someone for directions, but you barely heard one word. You were too distracted. Hearing requires us to focus—a skill in and of itself. To complicate matters, the mastery of hearing is only one element (albeit a key factor) of good listening. So now we've learned that the foundation of good listenership requires the ability to develop one's hearing skills.

If you stop reading this book right now and figure out for yourself how to hear (and listen) better, you will become better at everything you do. However, since there are proven techniques to improve hearing and listening skills, why not read on and learn them?

If you were only one of two people on this planet, would you be able to hear and listen to the other member of your two-person civilization? The obstacles to really hearing what is being said, and the obstacles to good listening, would still exist even in a two-person society. So, it's not hard to understand the difficulty when we interact in each of our own circles of friends and colleagues—our mini-societies.

Why is it so hard to hear effectively? Why is it so hard to be a good listener? Perhaps because we just assume we can do it well. Perhaps because we don't recognize the importance of developing these skills. As infants, we quickly learned that the key to our satisfaction—even to our survival—was "speaking," often as loud as we could. We somehow internalized that our sounds had the power to generate a desirable response from our parents, and sometimes, most of the time, we could bring them to us with our cry (discomfort) or keep them with us with our coos and giggles (pleasure).

Hence, as soon as we could utter sounds, hearing took a back seat to speaking. Our voice was far more useful than our ears. As we developed our verbal ability, we learned that it's "easier said than heard," and much "easier said than listened to." Any child psychology book will explain the various psychological and emotional underpinnings for why it is the case.

For a time, this behavior worked well for us. Society was kind enough to label this self-centered focus on speaking (crying), as the socially acceptable Terrible Twos. Yet, as we continued to grow, we began to develop our hearing skills. We learned that if we ate the not-so-tasty, healthful food, we would get to eat the delicious stuff. In other words, eat your vegetables and then you can have dessert. We also learned that if we were quiet and behaved well, we would be rewarded. Pavlovian response-reinforcement quickly taught us how to obtain the desired result.

LISTENING!

HEAR + OBEY = REWARD

So . . . even though we understood the simple equation, how come we failed so often to fully hear what was being said, even though the person speaking was:

- The only person speaking

- Right in front of us, or

- Had the power to make us comfortable or uncomfortable

"Well," you say, "we were just children!" True. Let's ask the question another way. Even though we (as adults now) understand the simple equation, how come we (still) fail so often to fully hear what was being said, even though the person speaking is:

- The only person speaking

- Right in front of us, or

- Has the power to make us comfortable or uncomfortable

The answer, of course, is that we simply were not (and still are not) listening. We might react to well-worn words and phrases, but we seldom listen. Psychologists are replete with reasons for poor hearing and listening skills. Fundamentally, it's about our ability to focus on the present and concentrate on what is being said at that moment.

However, focusing on the present moment is easier said than done, but fortunately, for the purposes of the skills discussed in this book, we don't have to do it all the time—just when it counts. You needn't study the Japanese Tea Ceremony or spend six months of meditation with Tibetan monks, although those disciplines would surely enhance your peace of mind and sharpen your hearing and listening skills.

Learn to focus on what is being said. Perhaps doing so all the time is impossible, but to do it when it counts is not so difficult. It just takes practice, and there are so many easy and fun ways to practice. Consider listening as a sport you wish to master. Just like any sport you want to learn, practice the required skills. So, too, with listening. You can start today.

Turn on the television and listen to the news. Concentrate on any story being covered at the moment. At the end of the story, turn off the sound and repeat the facts you just heard. Did you hear every word? Did you miss anything? Did you tune out? Did you get bored? Were there any distractions—doorbell, telephone, cat? What about the pictures? Did they help you concentrate or divert your attention from the focus of the story? Did the newscaster's face draw you in? Did you glance at the crawl at the bottom of the screen—the one identified as "breaking news" that had nothing to do with the story you were trying to listen to?

You get the point. Under the best of circumstances, there are distractions. Why, even Adam had trouble listening to the Creator, even though the only other person on the planet was Eve (who also didn't listen!). However, there was an upside. It immediately spawned the age of apparel—a positive by-product completely overlooked by students of biblical history. So, had there been no pictures, no crawl, no doorbell, no phone call—no other distractions—would you have heard everything the newscaster said? Probably not—not because of your ability to hear, but because of your ability to listen.

With practice, you can develop your ability to focus on the speaker's words and block out, or become oblivious to, external distractions. With practice, you will sharpen your ability to concentrate and focus. However, the more insidious distractions are internal. Our internal distractions sabotage us. They stop us from being in the present. Most of us are not good enough listeners to block them out, but with practice, we can develop the ability to block out internal distractions.

Daydreaming while someone else is speaking probably tops the list of internal distractions. Perhaps you are saying to yourself right now, "Hey, I'm bright! I can stop myself from daydreaming, if I need to." But haven't you daydreamed countless times in conversations, meetings and conferences—even if only for a moment? How do I know? Because I know that, from time to time, all of us mentally finish the speaker's sentence or turn off momentarily because we think we already know what the speaker is about to say. Or, perhaps we flash back to an unpleasant, unrelated personal encounter still festering within us, or fast forward to an upcoming event we're excited about. And since we think much faster than we speak, our thinking words drown out the other person's spoken words. Perhaps we are always dreaming, at least a little bit.

Listening 101

The first rule is to learn to hear all of what is being said. Make sure you hear the last syllable of the last word spoken in the speaker's every sentence. Imagine that you can see the period at the end of each sentence.

It's just like playing a sport. To be good at batting, golf, pitching or any other similar activity, we must follow through on the swing or the throw. Likewise, hearing well also requires follow-through. But in this sport, the follow-through is hearing all of the words—especially the last word—and the silent period at the end of each sentence. Did you hear that? You must hear the period that identifies the end of each sentence. This ability is an acquired skill for all of us. In order to be great at hearing what someone says, we need to hear the silence, to feel the space and time between words and sentences. When we do, we can really "get it."

Just as the proper follow-through in the swing of a bat or golf club must be learned because it is not a natural movement, so, too, must the proper follow-through for a listener be learned.

We have to learn first how to hear, and then how to listen, because listening was:

- not natural for an infant—babies don't understand language,

- not comfortable—we lost control (we thought) when we were not speaking, and

- not necessary, at least until we learned that our cooing or crying was no longer enough to obtain the comforts we wanted (or get the goodies).

Now, maybe you're thinking that hearing the last word of the sentence and the period that marks the silence between sentences is just too much to ask. But, it's actually quite easy once you master the technique. And not only is it easy, but it's worth it.

To return to the sports analogy, once you have mastered the stroke or the swing, from start to follow-through, your level of performance will be consistently better. I'm not saying that every stroke or swing will be perfect, but once you grasp the basics, things will only improve. You will have raised your game. For example, if a golfer takes 90 strokes to complete an 18-hole golf course, by golf standards not every stroke was well executed. Yet most of us would nevertheless consider a 90 to be a respectable score for a round of golf.

It's the same with hearing. Okay, you may not have truly heard every word, but you have heard more than before, particularly the words at the end of the sentence—the "throw-in words" or inadvertent slips that are often the most telling. Think of those throw-ins as your bonus for learning to hear well. What's so important about them? Sometimes they contain vital clues to the real intent of the speaker.

So how can we learn to hear better? Learn to:

- Block out external distractions (doorbell, telephone, spouse, lunch, _____).

- Block out internal distractions (worries, daydreams, plans, _____).

- Focus on the present and on what is being said to you, right then.

LISTENING!

- Listen for the ends of the sentences and for the silence between them.

Begin each conversation with the belief that what the other person has to say is important, and always assume you can learn from what he or she has to say. You will be taking a giant step towards perfecting your hearing skills and becoming a better listener. These skills are essential to becoming effective at virtually everything you do involving communication. You will enhance all of your personal interactions, and you will become a better parent, spouse, colleague, friend, and negotiator.

PRACTICE POINTS

- Listening isn't so easy. It requires focus and concentration. It's an acquired skill, requiring us to bear down mentally.

- Good listeners block out external distractions. Great listeners block out internal distractions as well.

- Always work to "hear" the silent period at the end of each sentence. Silence is golden.

- Let the speaker fill the silence. Often, that's when his true meaning and intent emerges via "throw-ins" and uncomfortable "add-ons."

Chapter 2

THE ART OF LISTENING

LISTENING!

Every successful person you know is a good listener (although he may not always be listening to you). To be a good listener, we need to use our ears, our eyes and, perhaps most important, our heart. Listening requires the use of our senses and a positive mental attitude that says to the world, "I want to understand and I am receptive." That receptive attitude will broadcast, "I am absorbing what you are telling me, because it is valuable."

Few of us are proficient listeners. We all can become good at it, but it's not easy. Let's take a look at the visual component of listening—use of the eyes. How often do we look, but not see? How often do we see, but not absorb?

Law enforcement departments nationwide require every officer-in training to study the techniques of observation. Why? Because to work in law enforcement, it is not enough just to see things. Candidates must develop the art of careful observation. It's one thing to see something; it's quite another to observe it—to really see it with all of our senses. For example, while strolling down a sidewalk, most of us will notice a person walking toward us or waiting for a bus. Some of us will also see all of the clothing that person is wearing, even an untied shoelace. Some of us will also notice what that person is doing, perhaps fidgeting with his keys. Yet, a few of us will also be able to see what that person may be feeling. Do they look anxious? Relaxed? Are they engrossed in a book? What book?

It's very much like the difference between hearing and listening. It takes focus and a desire to really look at someone. Few of us really do it—even when the person we are looking at is directly in front of us.

Speaking to us! The skill we need to master is learning to see with "all of our eyes."

In order to really see the other person, you need to look at him—to literally focus your eyes and your interest on the other person. In addition to being polite, it allows you to observe the speaker's body language. A shift in position, a nervous foot, pencil-tapping, and the like may telegraph an unspoken attitude or a self-betrayal. Does every movement have a meaning? No, but many do. It's generally in changes where unspoken clues are divulged, and unspoken words are spoken.

Changes in movement often become more revealing as the pressure between the parties intensifies. For example, have you ever noticed yourself become a bit itchy when you are nervous? Do you double-check to make sure an article of clothing is on just right? Or pat your hair, or surreptitiously check for a particle of food in your teeth, or indulge in any of the little frets and fears we're all prone to when we should be thinking of something else?

We can hear body language just by looking at one another. It's generally easy for the "active person"—the speaker—to discern whether the other person is hearing (some or all of what is being said), or listening. Getting it, so to speak.

Remember the last time you started a conversation with someone who was distracted? He looked away, stepped back, scanned the room, maybe smoothed his tie, and pulled at his cuffs. Perhaps you surprised or even offended him; perhaps he just wasn't ready to pay attention. This sort of behavior by the listener is fairly easy to understand. The listener is, at that moment, passive or reactive, because he is being spoken to and he may feel uncomfortable being focused upon. On the other hand, the speaker is in the physically active role. As a result, his body movements are secondary, upstaged by the words and their meanings.

It is the apparently unintentional behaviors that we should carefully observe and absorb. Involuntary body movements are our physical Freudian slips—excessive clearing of the throat, inappropriate glances away from the listener, jingling of change in the pocket—all are important ingredients to toss into the "blender" of the clues we hear, see, and sense as we reflect on and absorb the conversation and its meaning. Doing so enhances our ability to truly see and hear. We can really get what is being said, as opposed to just the words the other person is saying.

However, no matter how well you learn to hear with your ears, no matter how well you learn to see (and even to observe) with your eyes, you will not master the art of listening until you also learn to use your heart. Even though your heart has many other responsibilities—pumping blood to all of your organs, falling in love, falling out of love, falling back in love—it will also enable you to listen better, if you allow it. So, what's the heart got to do with it? Think of the heart as the center point of a vast web, where all of your other senses converge into focus. There, your senses bring what they've learned to be absorbed and understood. Our language is full of phrases underscoring our expansive concept of the heart: "have a heart," "use your heart," or "where's your heart?" The heart is the fulcrum of much more than the circulatory system.

I hope you understand the concept of hearing better—hearing all of each sentence. I hope you grasp the idea of seeing better—all through a focused attention. However, maybe you are struggling with the concept of listening with your heart. Yet, you've done it many times without realizing it. For example, have you ever sensed the next thing the other person would say, or the way the other person was really feeling even though they were trying to hide their emotions? Have you ever thought, or said out loud, "I know how you feel, or what you're thinking."

How did you know? It probably occurred with someone you knew well. You had an interest in that person, you knew the person's background, and you listened to him with all of your senses, including your heart. Hence, you were able to commune with him—feel in concert with him. As a former president once famously said to the public, he could "feel their pain." You will too—if you allow yourself to fully engage.

Best of all, you can listen with your heart not just to your friends and loved ones, but also to your adversaries, even complete strangers. All you need do is be receptive. Open up your heart and use all of your senses to listen to the other person. That is empathy. If you do, surprisingly often you will really understand the other person. Why? Because you listened. You were open to the seemingly hidden needs, wants, and desires of the other person. You empathized. And when you did—when you understood, and entered into, another's feelings—you moved toward becoming a worldclass listener.

In the parlance of late night infomercials, "But wait! There's more." By carefully listening, with the goal of understanding the speaker's point of view, we begin to understand his perspective. As a result, we begin to understand him. Moreover, when we allow ourselves to listen, we open ourselves to learning new facts, new perspectives, and new approaches. We may not agree with the speaker, but we cheat ourselves by not trying to understand him. When we understand what the other person is saying, we may then allow ourselves to adjust our approach to a particular issue or problem, or even be open to changing our mind. Not only is listening silently complimenting the speaker, it allows us the opportunity to learn. Listening then becomes learning and growing.

Many years ago when I was a young lawyer, I took a long lunch break to return a defective shirt I recently purchased at a local department store. At the returns window, I found myself at the end of a surprisingly long line. However, I had taken an extra half hour just in case there was a delay. The line moved slowly. By the time I was second in line, it was just about noon. I noticed there was no one behind me. They all had left. The reason? A sign indicating that the returns window closed for lunch from noon until 1:00 PM. The people behind me obviously had decided that waiting would be futile.

I, on the other hand, decided to visualize myself at the returns window before noon. It was just 11:55 AM and I was only one person away from the window. However, what I didn't expect was that the woman ahead of me would be trying to return a dress for full credit, even though it looked obviously worn. The clerk, a young girl, studied the dress and rightfully questioned the return. In moments, the conversation became heated and tempers began to flare. The return clerk, whose composure was transforming from calm, cool, and collected to upset and agitated, called her manager. At the end of the battle, it was almost 12:05 PM.

I could see that the clerk couldn't wait to escape to lunch break heaven. Nevertheless, I stepped forward. I knew that if I didn't find a way to return my shirt—right then and there—I would have lost precious time and would have to return on another workday or, worse, on a weekend, when the lines would be much longer. Not the end of the world, but something I wanted to avoid.

Now, I had been observing the clerk, and I could feel how upset she was. After all, I had witnessed the entire encounter. As I stepped up to the return window, I could sense what was coming. I knew she was about to utter the dreaded opening words, "I'm sorry sir, but . . ."

I needed to preempt that negative response. Why? Because basic human nature dictates that as soon as someone starts with a no, they become invested in that no. It's far easier to obtain a yes on a blank conversational slate than to obtain a yes after the other person responds with a no—even though a no may not really be a forever-no—but more about that in Chapter 5. I wanted an opening line to preempt hers—the dreaded, "I'm sorry sir, but . . ."

As she turned her gaze from the manager and the other customer (who was finally leaving) toward me, I looked her square in the eyes and said, "I can't believe what that lady was trying to do! She was so rude to you—I was so impressed with the way you dealt with her. I don't know if I would have done so well." I had personalized our encounter and created a mini-relationship (which is exactly what every negotiation and most communication is, regardless of length).

The truth is that she had not really handled it well at all. But I let her know that I "felt her pain" and before she could close her window, I thanked her for squeezing me in, even though she was already using up part of her lunch hour.

Now, I could have waited for her to tell me she was closing and then I could have argued, "How can you do that (to me)? I've been waiting 30 minutes!"—all in a bellicose or cajoling or victimized manner. Maybe, by bullying, I could have turned her no into a yes. But can you say, "uphill climb"?

Instead, I started at the top of the hill by visualizing a yes. What I observed was a young, frazzled clerk who was embarrassed and, therefore, wanted to—needed to—escape to behind-the-back-door heaven. Rather than attack, I joined forces with her. I felt her pain. That clerk was years my junior, but I related to her as my equal. We are all equals in life, even if not in society. No matter how the clerk may have perceived me in my business suit, I bridged any societal difference.

I assumed that she simply wanted to do a good job—and that she wanted to say yes. So I swore to her that I hadn't worn the shirt (it was pretty obvious), showed her a button that was chipped, and she accepted the return before she went to lunch. A successful negotiation was completed; my goal was achieved and everybody won. The return clerk finished her morning by doing her job and feeling good about it. She felt vindicated (by me) for holding her position against the prior customer, and I was able to return my defective shirt.

Had I not been listening to what was going on—had I not seen the clerk and other customer interact, had I not used all of my senses to feel the clerk's discomfort but instead "zoned out," perhaps I would have walked up to the return counter and been told it was closed. Perhaps I would have used brash words and an aggressive tone to try to get the clerk to keep the return window open—most likely, only to find her dig her heels into a no.

Instead, I personalized a meeting with a perfect stranger, in this instance someone many years my junior. I created a mini-relationship by understanding and sympathizing with her discomfort. By meeting her needs, she met mine. I furnished commiseration and compassion and a chance for her to say yes with a smile. In return, she accepted my shirt and felt good about taking care of a customer.

For now, what you should take away is that an important element of negotiation is the art of listening—getting information from the words of another—enabling you, the listener, to better understand the other's needs, wants, desires, and challenges. Of course, it's seldom that we can eavesdrop on a conversation. Therefore, to extract information, we must ask questions and listen (it's so important, two later chapters are devoted to this technique)—listen with all of our senses, listen with our heart.

As you learn to become a better listener by using all of your senses, you will understand more and more about the other person, both from verbal comments and, often more significant, from nonverbal comments. You will discover the other person's hidden wants and desires. Within the unexpressed needs and expectations lie his insecurities and fears, or true needs and objectives. This buried treasure trove of information will often be so obvious, once we learn to listen, that we will be surprised—surprised at how obvious it really is. Most surprising, it will happen as often as not.

Why? Because most of us talk too much. As a result, we often disclose more about ourselves—about our position or strategy (in a negotiation), about our marriage, about our aches and pains, about our life—than we realize.

How can we learn so much just by being a good listener? Simply because we are all human—not machines. Even the best of us can only camouflage our feelings and emotions some of the time. In fact, it's hard to hide our internal state of mind. Hiding our feelings requires us to act robotic—to act against our normal impulses to be human and express our humanity. If you are still unconvinced, just read the Israeli airport security training manual, much of which is being adopted by our airport security personnel. The interpersonal aspects of airport security—the questions and answers between security personnel and travelers and the nonverbal clues—are emphasized as crucial sources of information.

Since our learning will increase when they speak, it is essential to develop techniques to facilitate and expand the amount of time the other person—adversary, partner, team member, or stranger—is speaking. How do you do it? Ask questions. Then listen. It's axiomatic that your learning will be enhanced as a function of the other person's amount of time speaking. Whether it's a negotiation, a sales pitch, or a conversation with a friend, loved one, or colleague, the best way to learn about the other person and his needs and expectations is to ask questions. Gentle questions at first. Then, use the responses as a springboard to delve into those areas that interest you, have an impact on you, or are gateways to more information and insights. We have now touched upon a key to becoming a good negotiator: the technique of eliciting information. But, more about that later. Let's first finish discussing the art of listening.

For example, in the context of a business negotiation, a gentle question might address the weather, difficulties in the trip to attend the meeting, or the general economy—perhaps whether interest rates are likely to rise or fall or whether consumers look like they're gaining or losing confidence. These types of questions are noninvasive. They are intended to elicit a response just to loosen things up and lubricate the dialogue, a technique that can be referred to as the use of opening pleasantries.

A less gentle question might focus on something important to the other person—for example, "How's (your) business?" However, the response might be an evasive, "So-so." Often the question will generate a defensive response—either for negotiating purposes or because many tend to respond tepidly so as not to tempt fate if things are going well. People don't always say what they mean or believe. For whatever reason, they may only be saying what they want us to believe, or what they believe, or simply what they think is the "right" answer.

For example, say representatives from two companies are negotiating for the sale and purchase of a truckload of gadgets. At some point in the conversation, Sid, the seller, says to Pete, the buyer, "I am running out

LISTENING!

of gadgets. I can't sell the truckload for less than $10,000."

How is Pete to know if $10,000 is the lowest and best offer of the seller? Pete heard the $10,000 figure, but is it a take-it-or-leave-it number? If Pete simply accepts what Sid said—and he needs that truckload of gadgets, game over, he pays $10,000.

But how well was Pete listening? Were there any clues to allow him to determine whether Sid had room to reduce his price? Based on these facts, there is no way to know. Pete should continue the conversation, because he needs more information. He needs to ask questions—the "why, how come, and don't you think" line of questions—that will elicit responses from Sid from which he can gauge whether there is further negotiating room (a technique to be explored in the next chapter).

Let's see how Pete uses questions to try to obtain a lower price from Sid. Would Pete be doing the best he could for his business if he accepted Sid's $10,000 price as final? Of course not! Pete must probe Sid and prolong the conversation in order to try to find a basis to obtain a lower price; yet, Pete must do so without blowing the deal—without causing Sid to get to the point where he says, "That's it, I'm leaving. If you can't afford the $10,000, I'll find another buyer."

Pete's in a difficult position. Sid told him the gadgets are scarce right now, and that he is running out of product. Maybe Pete should first ask a question to confirm that key fact, but he cannot imply he does not believe Sid. Why must Pete be so sensitive in this probe? Because Sid did not imply he was low on gadgets, he clearly expressed it. If Pete was listening, Pete knows he must be careful not to question or attack Sid's integrity by implying that Sid lied or exaggerated. How can Pete dig into the issue without creating a sense of disbelief?

"How come you're running low?" Pete might ask. "What happened?"

Perfect! This should engender a response from Sid to explain why his company is running low on gadgets without implying a credibility issue.

Let's assume Sid's response is plausible. Now Pete is really jammed.

Pete needs to continue the conversation, but cannot bear down on the scarcity issue after Sid's plausible answer. To do so could suggest that Pete is questioning Sid's integrity. Therefore, Pete needs to introduce other bases to negotiate a lower price. Pete might offer to pay cash. If Sid pursues the all-cash offer, Pete may learn that Sid is a little cash-strapped. Or Pete might say that he'd be willing to delay the purchase for a better price in the future. He might find Sid amenable to a better price if Sid wants to lock in a future sale. Either approach allows Pete to continue the conversation and perhaps learn new facts.

If all else fails, Pete will need to fall back upon either his relationship with Sid or the relationship between their respective companies in order to get a better price. While Sid may not reduce the price, Pete's ability to get Sid to drop his price will be increased by continuing the negotiations. In most negotiations, leverage trumps negotiating skill. Good luck, Pete. Buying gadgets when they are scarce leaves little leverage, if any, for an anxious buyer.

PRACTICE POINTS

- We must use all of our senses to really listen. We need to see "with all of our eyes" to really get it.

- By combining our aural and visual senses with our heart, the speaker feels our interest, and will usually help us to understand his perspective or point of view.

- Never cut someone off. We learn from listening, not from speaking.

- Use questions to nudge out information. Combine questions with silence to open doors to the speaker's real intent and motive.

- Once we start speaking, we tend to divulge more than we intend or realize.

Chapter 3

ASK QUESTIONS . . . THEN, BE QUIET AND LISTEN!

LISTENING!

It's fascinating how often success is described with expressions of extraction. "You really hit pay dirt," we hear people say. "That deal is an oil well!" or even "There's gold in them thar hills." All of these expressions deal with the concept of extracting something of value. It's the same when speaking with someone.

How much more difficult would it be if we had to communicate with someone who wasn't speaking? Yet, that is exactly what we do when we dominate a conversation. How much harder must it surely be to understand another when the amount of information being offered, being extracted, is limited?

The key to extracting information is eliciting it. Elicit information by asking questions and then focus on the responses with a genuine interest (listening!). Most people disclose more than they think and, to the experienced listener, often say as much or more through nonverbal communication.

Sometimes, when a person is saying something that is difficult or painful, or not entirely true, or about which the speaker is unsure, his glance away is the nonverbal give-away. Sometimes it's a twitch, a tic, a throat-clearing, a nervous movement of a leg or foot, or scratching. None of these movements would have significance in a vacuum but, absorbed into the entirety of the conversation, they may provide clues to the speaker's true feelings. Just as a change in a patient's body is a clue to a doctor, changes in a speaker's physical position may signal the listener to detect clues for true meaning. Changes in intonation and cadence can also be important clues, and of course, the inadvertent verbal misstep (the famous Freudian slip) is virtually always the most revealing. However, these nuances can only help to understand the other side in the context of the words being spoken. So, let's return to the art of extraction.

Instead of using picks and shovels, derricks and backhoes, negotiators extract information and the answers they seek with questions.

We've all heard the adage that we are born with two ears and one mouth because we would be better served by listening twice as much as speaking. The bookstores are full of works on salesmanship. They all recognize that good salesmanship requires the ability to ask questions. But, in order to ask the right questions, we must listen to all that is being said. By listening to the responses, we can then ask clarifying follow-up questions to confirm our understanding. Why guess? By asking the right questions, the needs or problems of the speaker will be extracted. Think of asking questions as drilling to find oil. The deeper the drill, the closer to the oil. Of course, in order to hit oil, we must drill in the right direction—ask the right questions. This requires preparation. It may require us to learn about the other person's business or the industry segment in which the other person's business operates. On a personal level, it may require learning about the other person's financial situation or home life.

I have made individual and multi-person sales calls many times. Yes, lawyers make sales calls. We're all salesmen, at least to some extent. We are all selling something, whether it's a product, a service, or an idea. As lawyers selling legal services, we might have the occasion to assemble a team to make a sales presentation to a prospective client. I have participated in so-called beauty contests, where several law firms each meet with a prospective client. The least effective meetings were staged to require us to speak first—make a "cold" presentation. The best meetings occurred when the client allowed us to ask pre-meeting questions and learn about his needs before we made our presentation. Of course, the key question, stated or implicit, is always, "How can we help you, what are your needs?"

Beauty contests, by their nature, have many contestants and only one winner. Moreover, sometimes the decision-maker already has a good sense of whom he wishes to select. The best way to increase the odds of winning—and avoiding the costs of participating when the chances of success are very low—is to ask pre-meeting questions. The very questions asked below:

- What are your needs?

- Why aren't they being met by your current firm, your current supplier?

- How can we help?

These questions will extract information to enable you to better prepare. What's the point of bringing a hockey stick to a baseball game? Would you bring your labor and employment department to a pitch for technology business, or would you want to bring your best technology people?

It's almost impossible to ask too many questions. We can never embarrass ourselves by asking intelligent questions. They simply need to be asked in a spirit of wanting to hear more to better understand the other side's needs, wants, and desires. It is said that there are no stupid questions. It's true. However, there are questions that drill straight down to oil, while others just poke dry holes. The latter may not be stupid, but they waste time and may imply lack of preparation. The ability to ask good questions is not a divine right. It requires homework to learn the questions to ask.

Before I began practicing law, I worked on Wall Street as a securities analyst. I was lucky enough to have a wonderful mentor. One of the greatest pieces of advice he gave me was that success would come from learning to ask the right questions—that was the tough task. Then in typical Wall Street talk, he ended the advice with, "Anyone can look up the answers." I have learned through the years just how very right this mentor was. I never cease to be amazed at the information that can be extracted with a series of relevant questions asked with sincerity.

Oftentimes, the first response to a question is guarded. However, careful probing allows the questioner to drill to the core, or get near enough to enable the practiced listener to truly understand what is being said.

There are many ways to ask questions. When in doubt, start with noninvasive opening pleasantries. However, keep in mind that what is noninvasive in one context may be invasive in another. For example, let's assume you were to meet your adversary, Mr. Jones, in his office. Upon entering, you notice pictures of his family, a college reunion picture, and a model sailboat. (By the way—this is a chance to see with all of your senses, not just glance around. So, what do you really observe? Is there a woman in the picture? Is she his wife? Is she wearing a wedding band? How many children and grandchildren are posing? What college did he attend? Which reunion was it? Is the model sailboat indicative of building model sailboats as a hobby or is Mr. Jones a sailor?). Questions regarding his office décor can be used as a part of the introductory pleasantries.

On the other hand, such questions might be too personal or invasive if your first meeting is in a conference room. Upon entering the conference room, study it. Are there clues about the other person's company or culture? Is it Spartan or is it the Taj Mahal? What types of wall decoration are used? How old are the decorations? Does any of this matter? Who knows? It's too early to tell. However, as the meeting progresses, you may learn your adversary or one of his friends, colleagues, or loved ones decorated his firm or painted one of the pictures on the wall. If you can talk intelligently about decorating or art, you may have uncovered a delightful connection.

Let's say you and your client, partner, or team member visit Joe Retailer to sell him on your ability to analyze the relative success of each of his stores in order to develop a repositioning plan to rehabilitate or dispose of Mr. Retailer's weakest stores. Joe's company owns and operates a chain of 190 moderate-priced teen apparel stores. Joe called you because he recognizes that some of his stores are performing poorly. This is a difficult presentation for you, because it requires three painful things from Joe. He must accept the need for the analysis, he must be willing to admit mistakes, and then he must be willing to take what may be painful action to correct them. It's going to be a tough meeting. At some point you're going to ask Joe to bare his corporate soul. Moreover, because of your experience, you know that Joe will most likely have more problem stores than he will initially feel able to acknowledge.

On the surface, this scenario is non-adversarial, but it is nonetheless quite difficult because you must explain to Joe why he needs your help to solve his problems. Hence, you must understand Joe's hidden desires, needs, and fears. Joe may recognize he needs help. But what type of help? Should he reposition or dispose of poorly performing stores? How should Joe execute this turnaround plan?

One way to reach Joe's oil is to review the numbers. By reviewing the financials, you obtain objective information—which of Joe's stores are performing below average, or worse, losing money. With a request to review the operating performance of each store, it may appear to be an easy sale to convince Joe to purchase a full analysis of his chain and implement a curative strategy based on the analysis. However, the sole question is not, "May we study the numbers?" That question alone only elicits empirical information. It must be followed by questions regarding the impact of the closing of any specific store and the impact of a program of multiple store closings. For example, questions affecting impact that ought to be asked include:

- How would you like to deal with your employees?

- How will your bankers react?

- How will your competition react?

- Are you concerned about public opinion?

- If publicly traded, how will Wall Street react?

How would you know to ask these questions? By doing your

homework, you would gain an understanding of the retail industry in general and of Joe Retailer's business in particular. That understanding will help you develop relevant questions. Is Joe the architect of the store expansion program? Are you suggesting that you will partially dismantle his baby? Perhaps it was the work of his predecessor. Is the company a family-owned business? If so, is Joe a member of the founding family or not? Questions about company history may furnish important information. Listening with your heart will enable you to discern Joe's level of emotional attachment. Was Joe speaking with a loving reflection, or just the opposite—a numbers-crunching approach (with 20-20 hindsight) to what was historically done right and not so right?

By doing your homework, you will be sensitized to the emotional impact of your questions, and the best way to implement a course of action. As you listen to Joe, you will learn his expectations. Was he expecting the analysis and action to focus on, say, 10–12 stores of his 190-store chain? What questions will you ask to help him divulge other problem stores? What questions will you ask to help Joe understand that the scope of the analysis may need to be broadened?

What questions would you ask? If it's a publicly traded company, you should have already done your homework by reading through all of the public filings such as Securities and Exchange Commission 10-Ks, 10-Qs, and 8-Ks. Should you attempt to analyze all the problem stores initially, or use the "salami" approach (an approach only seeking one slice [an analysis of just a few stores] with later slices to follow as the facts suggest)? Is this approach really any different for any other type of negotiation; *i.e.,* asking questions to better understand all of the facts—financial, psychological, and emotional?

So you've just entered Joe's office, you've looked around and you're still stuck for an opening. Break the ice by recounting how the current meeting came to pass. Even if it's just recounting the series of telephone calls and e-mails that led up to the meeting. Recount those conversations and e-mails; use them as a springboard until you are ready to end the so-called opening pleasantries (which can include the "how are you, what's new, how's the weather, how's the family, and what do you think of the economy" icebreakers). You'll sense when the pleasantry stage should end.

Then, begin the substance of the meeting, but don't be so quick to do so. Once the substance of the meeting begins, it usually puts everyone in attendance on guard—people tighten up a bit. Therefore, you may wish to continue the opening pleasantries. This is often a good opportunity to gather more valuable information. Take your time with Joe—perhaps allow him to set the pace.

Let's look at another scenario. Say you represent a landlord. The two of you are meeting with a potential tenant and his attorney to discuss opening a retail store in your client's shopping center. The retailer owns a chain of boutique chocolate shops, and you're meeting to negotiate a lease for one of the retailer's proposed new stores. Your client would like a chocolate shop in his shopping center.

Having done your homework, you know the locations of many of the chocolatier's shops. You've studied how the retailer operates. However, you don't know how each store performs or how the overall company is performing because it's privately owned.

Part of your preliminary research might be to study the price of the cocoa bean over the past few years. Then, as one of the openers, you might ask, "Where do you see cocoa prices going? You're the expert." In one short sentence, you've praised the other side and opened with a relevant and noninvasive question. You might follow up with questions regarding the impact of rising cocoa prices. This is a quasi-invasive question since rising prices for raw material can't be good for a retailer. Yet, prices are public information. If prices rise, the retailer's cost of goods will rise. The question, of course, is whether he can pass the costs on to his customers.

These questions are intended to elicit a response—not a conversation. You should be asking questions and listening. Since you are inquiring about a topic that this retailer lives and breathes, he may be pleased with your interest. He may become quite responsive. Remember, once people start talking about themselves or their business, they generally say more than they realize. Don't cut them off—don't interrupt! All you need do is drill into the other side's oil well—their treasure trove of information—by lubricating your drill with questions. Then focus, and listen with your ears, your eyes, and your heart—your entire being. Be the receptacle—be the human sponge—of every piece of energy directed at you, whether by spoken word, inflection, or body movement. Understand the other person by absorbing their total presence. Be completely in the present.

If asking questions does not come naturally, then simply ask yourself:

- Why are you meeting?

- What is your goal?

- What is the goal of the other side?

- What would you like to know about the other side?

- How will you reach your goal?

- Who or what is necessary to achieve resolution and agreement?

Questions will come to you. If you are stuck, don't think of the meeting as a negotiation. Consider the meeting to be an opportunity to create and develop a relationship. In fact, that is exactly what you are doing—creating and developing a relationship. It may only last for a few weeks or months. Perhaps only until the deal is done. On the other hand, it might last for life. You will become comfortable and able to ask relevant questions if you have a sincere desire to form and develop a relationship by understanding the other side. That desire will reflect itself in spoken and unspoken ways. It will be clear to the other side. They will feel it. They will feel your interest and sincerity. Virtually every meeting initiates an incipient relationship among the participants. You can elect to allow the relationship that developed during the course

LISTENING!

of negotiations to wither and die, just as a plant will wither and die from lack of water. You can maintain the relationship at the level it reached when negotiations concluded or you can grow it by cultivating the seeds you have sowed and irrigating them with the water of communication.

It's a busy life; it's a complex world. It's up to you to select which relationships you will work to maintain or grow. The key is to recognize that every negotiation, no matter how short—say, only 30 minutes—is a relationship. See it as such and you'll improve your results. Open your heart to all encounters as mini-relationships. Then, all of your questions will be sincere. None will be offensive. Just adjust your attitude—don't let your ego show. Always let your heart show.

We'll return to the art of using questions later in the book, after we've digested some other concepts and techniques.

PRACTICE POINTS

- Questions set the direction. It seems counter-intuitive. Yet, it's the questioner who is in control.

- Questions are inherently complimentary.

- Questions create the platform for greater knowledge.

- Follow-up questions, graciously asked, show interest in what the speaker has to say.

- Questions combined with silence create a magnet to draw out facts plus true intentions and motivation.

- Well-asked questions are the drills to knowledge. The key is in the questions.

- Questions put the responder on the "stage of compliment" urging the responder to perform.

- Treat every meeting, every negotiation, no matter how short, as the beginning of a relationship.

- Negotiations are incipient relationships.

- The right questions get results. As Chris Matthews famously says every Sunday during his "Hardball" program, "Tell me something I don't know."

Chapter 4

EGOTUDE

Ego, which is the Latin word for I, is our sense of self-importance. Because our ego can be so detrimental in developing, maintaining, and enhancing a relationship, its negative impact deserves a special word to embrace it—egotude.

Think about how we feel when we speak with our ego. Are we speaking in a haughty manner, a disdainful manner, in a tone that causes the listener to feel demeaned? Isn't that exactly what we are trying to accomplish when we speak with our ego? We are expressing or implying a sense of superiority—a sense that what the other has to say is far less important than the pearls that will flow from our mouth. We all do this.

Worse, we do it not just with words, but our faces. And expressions can be more demeaning than words. We've seen it, we've heard it, and we've said it: "It was written all over his face!" Have you ever noticed the look on the face of a listener filled with egotude? You know the look I mean. The face of scorn, derision, and ridicule that broadcasts the listener's opinion: the speaker is not to be taken seriously. How often is the face of ridicule the response to our children?

We all are guilty of this from time to time. But how do we feel when we make those faces? Not so good. How can it be good when we're emitting negative feelings? Similar to how we feel after we lose our temper—not so good. It's because our ego causes us to say and do things that Edge Goodness Out of the moment—EGO. Our goodness escapes and dissipates when we allow our ego to surface, filling us with negativity. When our ego surfaces, it edges goodness out of the moment, perhaps out of the day—maybe longer. When that happens we, just as much as the recipient of our "egotudinous" attitude, become the victim; in fact, even more than the recipient, we suffer from the fumes of that attitude, because afterward we have to live with the erosion our ego has done to us and to them.

Resolve to let your goodness shine. Use your goodness to bury your ego by letting the trespasses of others roll off your back. Allow yourself to feel that what others have to say is worth listening to. Your success, on every level, will only grow if you let yourself listen— listen and hear with your heart. By listening and allowing yourself to understand the other side, you will naturally find solutions to solve both sides' needs. A negative attitude is always counterproductive. It's even more counterproductive when allowed to surface in front of others. A negative attitude not only blocks your ability to listen, but also it "chills" the other person. He will sense the lack of interest or lack of desire (or sense of superiority or demeaning manner) emitted by your negative attitude.

When starting a negotiation or any conversation, acknowledge and examine any negative attitude you may feel. Where does it come from and what is it aimed at?

Who: Your adversary, spouse, child, colleague and/or his position in the negotiation?

What: The negotiation itself? The issue at hand?

Where: The venue?

When: The time of day?

Why: Do you just not want to be involved?

Once you determine the direction of your irritation, you'll determine the source. Once you determine the source, you'll be able to neutralize it internally.

Perhaps your adversary (or child) is young, not very experienced, or has not been given the authority to make a deal and, right or wrong, he thinks the negativity is being directed at him personally. This will create a disconnect between you and that person, which is detrimental. Why? Because usually the only "connect" between business participants is their having to be at the same meeting at the same time to negotiate the same deal. Not always a strong enough "connect" to overcome any "disconnect."

No matter what's going on in your life or how your day has been going, no matter how annoyed or insulted you may feel at having to be there—being opposite a neophyte, being opposite a person with limited authority—why not leave your negativity at the curb? There is no point in dragging a negative attitude around with you, whether you're starting a negotiation with your adversary or a conversation with your spouse or child.

Why is it so difficult to shed a negative attitude? One word: Ego.

In fact, it is not difficult to shed a negative attitude at all. It's easy. It's as easy as changing your shoes.

When I was in the Boy Scouts, I read the official handbook many times. There was a section on hiking that included the admonition to wear comfortable shoes suitable for long hikes. After the warning, there were two pictures. One picture was of a happy boy scout; the other, a sad boy scout. The difference between them was their shoes. One was wearing "style" shoes—fashionable, but unsuitable for hiking. Perhaps his ego caused him to dress fashionably. The other was wearing "smile" shoes. Not so great-looking, but comfortable and suitable for hiking. Perhaps he was able to control his ego and just be himself.

It's the same with attitude. Which attitude are you wearing right now, as you head into your next meeting or walk into the office? It's simply up to you. Dress yourself in a positive attitude. Leave the negative attitude in the closet. Slip into the "smile" shoes. They look good on you!

If a negative event occurs, get through it. Keep in mind that for the most part, you don't need to take someone's remark or action—however annoying or ill-mannered—personally. Just deflect it, let it roll off and away, and wrap yourself in that positive attitude.

If it is so easy to change attitudes—really just like changing shoes, and even easier if they are loafers not requiring lacing—why do so many of us get caught up in negative attitude? Because when our ego is bruised we catch a case of egotude. Yet, the odds are high that whatever bruised our ego was unintended. Often, we interpret an action or inaction—say, failure to include us in a meeting or copy us on an e-mail or otherwise keep us in the loop—as intentional when it isn't. Even if we know it was just an oversight or an accident, we take it as an insult, because we consider ourselves to be too important to have been overlooked.

Have you ever felt that way? Of course you have. Did you let it spoil your hour, day, or week? Even worse, did you blow up and allow it to almost spoil your career? That experience was a test, one of countless tests of your ability to succeed.

Did you allow your self-esteem, your internal grace, to control your ego and get over the hurt? If so, you felt better quickly. And you passed the test.

Or, did you allow that wound to your ego to fester? Did you mention it to others, seeking their support? What did you accomplish? You convinced yourself you were right to be upset. The more you fed your ego by convincing yourself how wronged you were, the more your irritation grew until it spiraled out of control and left you with the booby prize—a stomach full of acid.

Who benefits from that internal drama? No one, least of all you. So when you are about to start a negotiation or any conversation, what shoes will you be wearing? The lightweight shoe that gives you breathing room and flexibility or the heavy boot that signals you are ready to use your weight and strength of egotude—the weapon?

The ego is the negotiator's nemesis. Egotude creates walls. Walls hinder us from reaching the other side. Our ego stops our heart from connecting to another person. Egotude speaks so loudly that we can't understand what the other side is saying. Egotude is always trying to sabotage us. The problem is that egotude is not always so easy to overcome. Worse, egotude divulges itself to others in insidious ways—ways of which we are often unaware or which we realize only in retrospect.

Remember what we've learned about developing our listening skills? Good listening requires observation of the other person's face—listening with our eyes for seemingly involuntary little changes in expression. Why? Most of us are sufficiently aware of our large muscle movements. Hence, we assume others notice as well. For example, we all assume everyone notices us cross or uncross our legs, or lean in, or other deliberate movements. However, the small, fleeting actions provide the best clues to your adversary's thoughts. A change in the tightness of the lips may reveal surprise or shock or (due to egotude) scorn. Think of your own face when you see a stranger do something foolish. Picture that look of scorn.

You can—and you should—conceal that look when your adversary says something you think is ignorant or foolish or immaterial. But better yet, you can—and you should—learn to transcend your feelings, not simply hide them. What can you possibly gain by showing a face full of egotude? How could that possibly enhance the deal? How can it possibly enhance you and your day?

"What goes around, comes around." Have you ever heard that? Do you believe that what you receive in life is often a function of what you give? If you believe that what you get is what you give, lose the look of derision, neutralize your ego.

On the other hand, when we exude a desire to connect, we improve our chances of connecting. If we radiate our desire to understand, we improve our ability to enlist the other side to help us by giving us what we both need—the information and impetus to offer suggestions and craft solutions. The surprising secret is that we virtually always will receive a multiple of what we give out, a gift from the ever-expanding universe.

Let's take our new skills out for a spin. You arrive for a meeting, without egotude, ready to do business or solve the problem. It is obvious, however, that the other party has a bad case of ego. As soon as you meet, you sense it in the offhanded way in which you are greeted. You have two distinct options.

Option #1 is to react in kind. You can think that the other person:

- Has no right to act superior

- Is being a jerk

- Doesn't know who I am

- Thinks of either me or my company or my clients as a "nothing"—barely worth dealing with

- You fill in the blank

Option #2 is not to react.

Instead, you can keep your egotude in your pocket. Keep the attitude you arrived with. Continue to wear your positive attitude. Recognize that the other person is having a bad day—regardless of the reason—and say to yourself, "That's okay!" Then, respond with grace and kindness. Unless he tells you, you won't know the reason for his egotude—his negative attitude. Ironically, when most people complain about what's bothering them, it's often not the real problem. Often, it's only a momentary false issue and not the underlying problem. The underlying problem may be either too painful or too personal for them to verbalize even to themselves, much less to you.

How can you diffuse someone's egotude? Use kindness. Show an interest in the other person by asking questions. Most important, recognize the situation. Do not react in kind. A reaction in kind will enflame the moment, and it could defeat the purpose of the meeting and derail the deal. If it's a conversation with your spouse or child, it may simply slam the communication door shut.

When egotude surfaces in our adversary, we need to work extra hard to control our own ego. The chances are that your adversary's initial responses to whatever you say will be short, curt, nasty, demeaning, or dismissive. So what! His responses can't affect you. His responses are merely a reflection of his current mood.

Rather than deepen the darkness of his mood, let's break down the wall of ego your adversary has built for himself. As discussed, opening pleasantries can elicit valuable information, but only if the room is not infected with egotude. If it is, your first move is to lance the boil of negativity and alleviate the pressure of that swollen ego. Use the opening pleasantries to delve into something the other side is known for or proud of—something they would like to talk about—with the technique of expressed or implied compliment. Use authentic curiosity. You might say: "My colleague mentioned to me that you are a terrific violinist," (or golfer, or serious art collector, or whatever—you fill in the blank). Just be sincere (offering an unlinked compliment to someone suffering from egotude will be perceived as patronizing).

Preparation sets the table of opportunity. If you did your homework, you already know a little about your adversary. With the number of Internet search engines available, and the amount of information available, it has become easier than ever to learn about any topic, including any person or company. This may be the opportunity to effectively use that information. Listen to those negative flies; then, catch them with your homemade honey.

The point is that you need to find ways—without being artificial—to personalize the meeting. This allows you to create the beginning of a relationship. Like it or not, you will be in a relationship with your adversary until the deal is done, and maybe for much longer. Why not work to make it deep enough to understand your adversary's true needs, fears, and desires? Then, you'll know enough, and be smart enough, to craft solutions. You'll be able to reach an agreement that may even be better for you, even if better just means that you closed a deal that might have been delayed, or worse yet, killed under an avalanche of egotude.

PRACTICE POINTS

- Our EGO "Edges Goodness Out" of us.

- Our ego allows our fears, insecurities, and weaknesses to surface.

- Our ego sabotages us whenever allowed to be unleashed.

- Let perceived trespasses pass. Most of the time it's only our ego that's hurt. In fact, most of the time the trespasses are unintended.

- Suppress the ego. Let insults go. Maintain a positive attitude. We are only hurt by perceived hurts if we chose to be hurt. Even if intended, trespasses only reflect poorly on the trespasser.

Chapter 5

NO! THE ANATOMY OF NO

There is a movie called "Congo" in which an expedition is sent to find a group that vanished seeking treasure in a legendary lost city. Maybe you saw it—I've seen it twice on television. It's a trite story line replete with a charismatic and grizzled super-guide, a strong-willed and brave female scientist, a victim-like male scientist, and crazed super-strong gorillas protecting the lost city and its treasures. All irrelevant to the point I'm about to make, but all of the ingredients for a mindlessly entertaining movie. But you didn't buy this book because of my taste in movies.

I mention this film because there is a scene in which the second group learns that one of the first expedition's members is nearby, but according to a local tribesman, the man is dead. The super-guide, steeped in all ways of jungle survival and knowledgeable in the culture and language of this particular tribe, explains in wise and compelling super-guide fashion that in the language of the local tribe, the word "dead" has many meanings—there are many levels of dead. In case you decide to see the movie (based, perhaps, on what I've told you here), I won't disclose the rest of the plot.

The point of the scene is simple and incredibly relevant. The local culture had only one word to describe the condition of the first expedition member: dead. Yet, they recognized many gradations. So, too, with real world humans. We only have one word for no—whatever the language. However, the word has countless gradations and meanings.

The good news is, if you ever have dealings with that local tribe, don't assume "dead" means eternally expired. Likewise, don't assume that here in the real world "no" means an eternal no. In fact, very few no's are eternal no's. Once you receive a no, you have endured the worst. Yet, nothing about you has changed. You're still okay. You only change if you allow yourself to become infected by the no; if the no reignites your fear of failure or rejection, you stop trying for a yes. You are no better or worse, smarter or not, than you were just before receiving the no. Therefore, when you negotiate for anything, don't necessarily assume a no is a final no.

Think of no as one of the following:

- No, not now.

- Maybe.

- No, based on what you have said—what you have offered.

- No, based on the facts as I understand them.

- No, based on my perceptions.

- No, because I am reacting to your egotude (or because I am filled with egotude).

- No, because you aren't even listening and trying to understand my needs, wants, desires.

Perhaps you think that to ask again is too pushy. Perhaps you think you will be too embarrassed to endure the rejection of a repeat no. It's our fear of no that creates the fear of rejection. That fear spawns some of the saddest sentences and thoughts in the universe—the ones starting with the plaintive words, "If only . . . ," the opening phrase of a lament for a lost opportunity.

Fear of rejection is perhaps the greatest obstacle to our happiness and success. All too often, it prevents us from reaching for what we desire. The fear of rejection is a prison for many of us. Its sibling is the fear of failure. Between these siblings there is no rivalry. In fact, they work in harmony to keep us locked in the prison of an unrewarding, unfulfilling status quo of frustration. These siblings seek to shackle us into a life of quiet desperation.

But, we can free ourselves. This prison has no guards. Its door has no locks. Just open the door and walk out. We just need to open the door inside our mind. This door is our fear. Fear of rejection or failure. Fear of the embarrassment of what others might think or say. But, should we care? Of course not!

Imagine if the world's great scientists feared rejection, if they allowed scoffing by the scientific community at their failures or beliefs to terminate their quests. We might still be rubbing sticks together to make a fire (see the Boy Scout Handbook—you can do it with determination and a willingness to risk a blister). We'd still be dying of minor ailments, and using typewriters.

Thomas Alva Edison, credited as the father of the light bulb, was asked why he continued with his experiments after so many failures. "I have not failed," he said. "I've just found 10,000 ways that won't work."

Books about salesmanship always assure us that a failed sales call merely puts the good salesman one step closer to his next successful sales call. Trite, but true.

Even public servants meet with obstacles. One man, whose name will be familiar to you, ran for a seat in his state legislature, but was defeated. Years later, he ran for a seat in the United States Congress, but was defeated. He tried again for the United States Congress five years later, but was defeated. He sought a seat in the United States Senate, but was defeated. He ran again four years later for the United States Senate, but was defeated. Later, he became the sixteenth president of the United States, Abraham Lincoln. He was also the only president to patent an invention.

Baseball is this entrepreneurial society's favorite pastime, maybe because it is just like real life. You only have to hit the ball safely one out of every three or four times. As your batting average approaches 300—not even one hit out of three at-bats—you are on the path to the

Hall of Fame. How good would it be if the commissioner of life told all of us that we just needed to be successful one out of every three or four attempts! Well, you are the commissioner of your life. Just tell yourself that two out of three failures is great, three failures out of four is just fine. In fact, one success out of hundreds may be all you need.

Whether in a baseball game, a sales call, an interview for a job, or a meeting with your boss for a salary review or promotion, what does it take to get hits? Hitters take batting practice, stretch, do calisthenics, and then swing the heavy bat in the batter's circle. But, the very best (or those in a slump) arrive at the ballpark early and stay late in order to take extra batting practice. So, too, the great golfers spend an hour or more at the driving range after they finish their round, especially if they are in a tournament. To think that you don't need to practice is arrogant. It is egotude. If unchecked, that sense of entitlement, stemming from your acute case of egotude, allows you to foolishly walk into the boss's office unprepared.

But, haven't you just entered into a negotiation? Of course you have. Have you prepared by thinking about your boss's needs, wants, and desires? What might your boss consider valid reasons to reject your request? Have you tried to understand how your boss perceives you? How might you see things if you were in his shoes? For example, how will your raise or promotion affect the other staff members and your boss's overall budget? Can you make a case for why your batting average allows your boss to give you that raise or promotion? How have you helped your boss distinguish you from others, or better yet, use your successes as an example to others?

This line of thinking is not about defeatism. You deserve the raise or promotion. This exercise is about understanding your boss's perspective so that you can help him grant your request. You say it's not necessary, he should know all that, you've been underpaid for years. Blah, blah, blah.

Let it go. Nobody, except your ego, cares about the insults you think you've endured. Just let it go. Reflecting on perceived injustices simply feeds the Petri dish inside you that is just waiting to incubate a virulent strain of egotude. What if you've never approached your boss or dread doing so because of your fear of rejection, your fear of failure? We all learned those fears early in life, so don't beat yourself up for having them, and don't imagine you don't have them, at least some of the time.

In seventh grade, I had the good fortune to be in Ms. Jeffers' homeroom. She was also my English teacher. She was smart, and I thought she was beautiful, like a movie star. I was dashed when she announced her engagement to Mr. Amos, a high school history teacher. I'll bet I wasn't the only seventh grade boy who was heartbroken—but I digress.

The real joy of my seventh grade existence was having the astounding good fortune to be seated, quite by accident, next to Nancy. I thought she was the prettiest girl in the entire seventh grade. Yet, I couldn't summon up the courage to ask her out on a date. Week after week, month after month, as the school term slowly evaporated, I sat next to her unable to ask her out. I was afraid of the dreaded no.

Finally, I summoned all of my courage and popped the question. She said no.

To me, that was the final level of no—the real, final, absolute, eternal no. My chance for happiness was dead, or so I thought.

I wish I could offer you a better ending . . . I tried again, we bumped into each other in high school years later, we found ourselves at camp together, or at college, or in the same firm. No, it didn't happen. Rather, I allowed that no to become eternalized and I never asked her out again. Opportunity lost, nascent love unrequited, my first "if only . . ." living with me every day for the rest of seventh grade.

"Cute story," you're thinking, "Sad, but trivial."

I've got a lot of no stories. Let me tell you a few others.

In the Boy Scouts, I yearned to become a patrol leader. I asked again and again, but I was always told no. Now, no one said, "No, you are too young" or, "No, you don't have enough experience" or, "No, wait until your patrol leader is promoted to senior patrol leader" or, "No, wait until you start earning merit badges." It was just a no. Yet, somehow, I must have sensed that those responses were not an eternal no. I worked and waited until I was appointed patrol leader. No became yes. Okay, still a child's story.

So, let's fast forward to my first job after graduation from law school. I became a securities analyst for a then-famous brokerage. I was earning a whopping $15,000 a year back then, and I quickly realized that the road to increased income was in sales. So, I obtained my sales license (as a registered representative) and used my spare time to telemarket for clients. I told myself that if I was able to obtain a meeting from one call out of every ten, I would be doing well.

I learned early that the easiest sell is to sell your colleague—the other guy's ability. It's a humble but effective selling technique. First, I literally looked up the telephone number of virtually every major corporation headquartered in New York City. Then, I called them to present my vision of the best private money management companies with whom they could invest the assets comprising their benefit plans. My plan was to have them invest a portion of their pension or profit sharing funds with the best of these companies, and I would work with them to constantly weed out the weakest and add more of their funds to the strongest. I knew I would earn commissions from the money management companies if I was successful in increasing their asset base.

My telephone rejection rate was staggering. The effort often seemed fruitless. Thoughts of giving up were always lurking, yet I kept cold calling. Over 100 calls produced three meetings. Those three meetings produced not one sale to a corporate benefit plan. However, I did land one large investor and, as they say on Wall Street, "he was a whale."

I was a success. Everyone in the office congratulated me. No one knew how many failures I endured, and no one cared. I had made scores of telephone calls. In baseball terms, I had struck out, a batting average barely above .000. My batting average was 1 for 137. Yet, I was a success.

From this experience, I learned one of the great lessons of life. It will hold for you as it has stood the test of time for me. Others remember only our successes. Failures evaporate like the morning dew. Perhaps you have scoffed at the failed attempts of others to accomplish their goals. I know I used to scoff. When I was younger, I saw the failures of others as foolish. However, I eventually began to understand that success is only measured by successes, not failures. My epiphany was the recognition that a few successes, even just one success, can overcome countless failures.

To some extent we all fear the response of no. But if the worst the other person can say is no, that's not bad at all. Remember, there's a high likelihood it's not a forever no. It may be a maybe, or a "no, unless. . . ." However, to understand the gradations of no, we must draw out the reasons and find the hidden location of the maybe or the unless. Then we can understand it and craft a way to turn the no into a yes.

Oh, but you feel the no is a rejection you can't endure, perhaps because it may be accompanied by derision, a raised voice, or other demeaning jab and you don't want to endure that again, particularly in front of others. Perhaps you're fearful the other side will yell at you if you probe the no. Have you ever been the subject of another's mini-rampage, full throttle with raised voice? Have you ever been personally attacked in front of your superior, your client, your girlfriend or boyfriend—whoever? I ask, who was the fool? The fool is the person who loses his temper and loses control (a concept to be discussed later—it's a big deal concept). It was not you. The fool is the person whose egotude escaped. Understand that those who act with arrogant superiority, perhaps combined with a dose of derision and loss of temper, are either insecure and/or carrying trespasses from others (how sad).

So, what do you do? What can you do? What should you do to restabilize the negotiation and, if you are so inclined (and you should be, unless your egotude is rising), save the meeting? All attendees are in the negotiating room for the same reason. To do the deal. Why waste the time already invested just because the other side had a momentary breakout of jerkiness?

There are many ways to save the other side from itself. If you don't, the other side may continue to fester, invest in its anger, and further try to justify the foolish outburst. That outburst is like a bullet being shot from a pistol. Once fired, it's truly spent. The worst has been shot at you. But you are still in one piece, albeit perhaps startled by the outburst. Okay, so what to do? It's simple.

Do not respond to any part of the attack. Take a deep breath. Maybe a few. Wait a few seconds (they will seem like minutes). Then, in your lowest audible voice—yes, your absolutely lowest, calmest, audible voice—perhaps express that you are sorry that whatever you said was taken by the other side as offensive.

But, you say, you'd never do that—never stoop to that level.

It is not stooping—at all. It's only your ego thinking you are. Keep your egotude in your pocket. Try this approach whenever someone "throws their ego at you," perhaps that garage mechanic who snickers, or the receptionist who speaks derisively when you ask for an appointment. Let the snickers and derision roll off your back. Snickering and derision are two ways in which the insecure exercise their need to feel superior. When you respond with kindness, you enhance your ability to get what you want. More importantly, you have shown compassion.

If you feel attacked by a scornful no, disregard the scorn and just take the words at face value. Then, in the gentlest, quietest, most respectful manner, ask that receptionist who derisively told you that Mr. Jones was too busy to see you if she would keep your telephone number so she could call you in case Mr. Jones has any cancelled meetings. Perhaps suggest, or just imply, that it's an opportunity to prevent her boss from potentially wasting open time.

You have just fed her superiority. So what? It cost you nothing. Even better, you have helped her do her job more effectively. You have offered to fill any cancellation. You have just helped her. You have given her a chance to move from a no to a conditional yes. A yes if a cancellation develops. The same psychology applies to the screaming adversary. By speaking gently and quietly, you help him to calm himself. To change attitude. By so doing, you improve the atmosphere to do the deal. By responding with grace, you have helped yourself.

Now, let's move from the fears of rejection and failure (spawned by prior no's) which mentally manifest themselves as the illusory locks on our internal gated prisons. Let's discuss Yes. Let's turn "if only" into "I did it!"

PRACTICE POINTS

No one enjoys saying "no." In fact:

- A "no" is seldom immutable. Treat a "no" as an objection, not a rejection.

- Look for the hidden "because" behind the "no" so you can transform it into a "yes."

- Think of a "no" as a "maybe later."

- Use questions to find and solve the objection or the reason for the "maybe."

Why not:

- Live a life free of "if only." Rejection is physically painless. Only our ego suffers from rejection if we allow it.

- Treat rejection as a learning experience.

- Don't allow the fear of rejection or the fear of failure to stop you from trying. Live your life in the batter's box, not the dugout. If you keep swinging, you'll hit the ball.

- Success is measured by successes, not failures. Failures evaporate like the morning dew.

Chapter 6

YES! THE "SMILEY FACE"

LISTENING!

Much has been written by many about how to obtain a yes, generally in the context of completing a sale. But the need to reach a yes applies in virtually every aspect of life. The reason we don't think about it so much—we don't focus on it so much—is because the failure to get a yes is often perceived as just an inconvenience. Yet, while many yeses eventually follow an initial no, a delayed yes often has a real cost. Time, as we often say, is money, and sometimes a delayed yes can be expensive, not just inconvenient.

Say you want your car tuned up. You call Gerhardt for an appointment for your highly engineered foreign automobile. He dutifully takes the call and offers an appointment in two weeks. A day that is inconvenient. You request a different day. He responds with an appointment in three weeks. You are upset because your car is already beyond its stated maintenance date. Moreover, the alternate date is also inconvenient. What you seek is an immediate appointment. The promise of a tip won't help. Gerhardt is expensive; he doesn't need and won't accept a tip. Now you are in a negotiation—trivial perhaps, with no real cost, unless you value your time and convenience. What are your potential moves? How can you persuade Gerhardt to say yes? How do you obtain an earlier and convenient appointment?

The first rule of yes is to recognize that all of us want to say yes. Unless someone is so overwhelmed with their own problems, they (i) want to do their job well and, (ii) more important, they want to say yes. Why is it that the first rule of yes is to recognize we all have a natural desire to say yes?

To understand why, take a reading break, and follow these instructions.

- Find a mirror large enough for you to see the reflection of your entire face.

- Say No. Until you say no in a normal manner—and you'll know when—keep repeating the word No.

- Say Yes. Then, until you say yes in a normal manner—you'll know when (when you stop laughing)—repeat the word Yes.

- After repeating the word yes until you feel you are saying it in your normal manner, slowly alternate the words no and yes. Don't rush. Say each word slowly and clearly.

Spend a minute or two—right now—doing this, then have a good, well-earned laugh, and come right back. I'll be waiting for you.

Interesting, huh? Did you learn a few things about no and yes?

For one, the word yes virtually requires you to smile. Saying the word no sort of draws your face—you—into yourself. Did you laugh with yourself when you said yes? Did you rather enjoy looking at yourself saying yes? Didn't you feel happier and better about yourself when you said yes? Well? Admit it! You did. If you don't think so, try it again.

On the other hand, saying no was simply not fun. You didn't look happy, did you? All your smile lines disappeared. Your entire facial expression physically changed into a no—a big negative. So, if yes brings a smile, and if smiling is something we all like to do, then we all must have an innate desire to say yes. We all want to feel happier.

Saying yes is a double win. It's a double positive because the person saying yes is smiling and the person at whom it is directed is seeing a smile. Perhaps the best way to elicit a smile from another is simply to smile at them. It's contagious! By seeking paths to yes, we rid ourselves of arrogance. Arrogance enflames our egotude and begets futility and self-erosion. If we walk the "smiley path" to yes, internally we build, piece by piece, the mosaic within us which leads toward harmonization between ourselves and the universe. The smiles reverberate within us, touching every aspect of our being with positive feelings. Harmonization may be a never-ending journey, but it is one worth taking.

It is foolish to fear a no, especially when virtually every no is, in some manner, changeable to a yes.

So, how do we get a yes from Gerhardt? Is it okay to make up a little story—a little white lie? For example, would you consider saying, even if it's not true, that you will be taking an extended car trip with the family next week (when in reality it will be next month)? You goofed up by not calling sooner, and now you're in a real pickle. Can (should) your morality live with the white lie? Is it justifiable because the alternative is great inconvenience? Is it a good negotiating tactic? My answer is no—a lot more about exaggerations and lies later.

However, assuming you can live with the hyperbolized truth, what was embedded in your white lie that might have evoked an earlier yes? First, you admitted your humanity. You told Gerhardt you goofed up, something with which Gerhardt could empathize. Second, you asked for his help because you need it not just to help yourself, to protect your family. Now, that's a heart-wrencher that tempts even the cold-hearted Gerhardt into wanting to be a hero by saying yes. Chances are that the forces of positivity, coupled with his innate humanity—his desire to say yes and to be liked—would have moved Gerhardt to at least try to help you with an earlier yes. The beauty of the equation is that Gerhardt gets to do his job better, gets the internal psychic reward of saying yes, and gets your grateful positive feedback, and you get your earlier appointment.

As for your morality, pray to atone for the white lie and resolve to avoid such tactics again. Exaggerations and lies exact a heavy toll. Work a little harder to get the same result with honesty. Your karma will thank you. Living a lie, even just an exaggeration, partially removes us from the reality of our life. The best way to obtain a yes is the honest way. By doing our homework. By preparing, we will be able to ask the questions that lead us to understand the other side's needs, wants, and desires. By removing the obstacles to making a deal, we will find a way to reach yes.

So, Rule #1 is to recognize that we all really want to say yes. Saying no is not fun (and a vindictive no is not only not fun but also stirs the acid of "mean and nasty"). How many times have you received a no coupled with a sad or embarrassed face, or a no followed by "I'm sorry" or "I wish I could do more."? Saying no is contrary to our human nature. So, overcome your fear of receiving a no. It's almost always, really, "No, but try again" or a maybe. Just a stepping-stone to your next yes. Get over the no. Think positively and keep working to reach yes.

Recalling the baseball analogy brings us to Rule #2. Unlike baseball, Rule #2 advises that there are no umpires and there are no outs in the game of life. Each of us can endure endless failure and rejection, just like Edison. Just try to understand why you were rejected or why you failed, and work harder. Start by agreeing with yourself not to give up. No one cares about your rejections and failures. Consider them a learning experience. A lesson of what experiment not to duplicate as you search to find the formula for your light bulbs. All that people will remember are your successes: that deal, that new client, that new customer, that great conversation with your spouse or child. So work towards yes. Work towards success. Don't let rejection or failure lock you into the status quo.

There simply are no outs in the game of life. You can stay at the plate and keep swinging indefinitely. In fact, after you've hit the ball once, keep swinging—it gets easier with practice. Don't worry about strike-outs (we are entitled to limitless no's). There are no umpires. No one can force you into the dugout. Only you can take yourself out of the game. You are your own team manager. As your own manager, always tell yourself to keep your head in the game and keep swinging.

LISTENING!

"But," you say, "I just keep striking out time after time! It's useless."

Nonsense, it's not hopeless. Go to the batter's circle. Practice your swing and your follow through (your approach). Coach yourself to improve your swing by better preparing for your next time at bat. Do you know the questions to ask? Are you sufficiently prepared? Are you allowing yourself to suffer from egotude? Do you talk too much and not listen enough? Most important, do you listen with "all of your heart and all of your might" so you understand what the other side is really saying?

Last, do you ever bench yourself during the negotiation or meeting? Could you have tried harder? Have you ever mentally taken yourself out of the game because your egotude got the best of you? Have you ever bobbled the ball? We all make mistakes—admit them and move on! Did you ever just freeze up and stay in the dugout? It's only your fear of rejection or failure—get through it! Walk out and get up to the plate! There are no outs in the game of life. Pick yourself up, dust yourself off, and wait for the next pitch. There are limitless at-bats. You'll eventually find a fastball you can hit for at least a single—maybe even out of the park. Remember most successes are simply due to perspiration and perseverance.

PRACTICE POINTS

We all want to say "yes":

- It's human nature to prefer to say "yes," rather than "no."

- Most "no's" can be converted to "yeses."

- We can endure countless no's and countless failures. There are no strike-outs or knock-outs in the game of life.

- You are your own umpire. You are your own team manager. Never strike yourself out. Never bench yourself. Keep playing. Keep reaching for "yeses."

Chapter 7

UNDERSTANDING

So far we have addressed:

- Enhancing our hearing skills

- Learning how to listen

- Using questions to learn about the other's needs, wants, and desires

- Putting our egotude in our pocket and keeping it there so it doesn't hinder our ability to listen or sabotage us in other ways

- Saying no for most people is uncomfortable and makes them squirm, just as, on the other hand

- Saying yes is a quite pleasant experience, and one which most of us will seek to do

- That most no's are convertible to yeses if we work to understand the reason for the no, and maintain a desire to change it to a yes

Our attitude is like a pair of shoes. The right shoes look good, they feel good, and because they look and feel good, we do, too. Other people notice and they react.

No matter what the circumstances are, we should always ensure we are wearing the right attitude. Attitude creates the frame of mind that negotiation is fun. Our attitude reveals that we are looking forward to success. Attitude broadcasts our desire to understand what the other person—an adversary, our momentarily agitated spouse or our overly excited or temporarily sullen son or daughter—has to say. We have learned that negotiation is the formation and maintenance of a relationship, whether momentary, an hour, a day, or longer.

When we think in those terms, we create positive attitude. It causes us to seek to understand the needs, wants, and desires of the other side. We just need to start with a "solver's" attitude, seeking to craft a way to make the deal, to solve the issue at hand, and create a win-win mosaic.

How can we do that if we are wearing a negative attitude? Remove the negativity by starting with an attitude that says, "How can we help each other?" This positive approach will only be undercut if we attempt to "sell" our ideas, our predetermined position, without regard to the other person's needs, wants, and concerns. If, however, we approach negotiations with the intent to solve the other person's problems and needs, our attitude will be perceived as positive and helpful. The other side—your spouse, or a friend, colleague, or stranger—will sense it and be more likely to react in kind. Start right now thinking in terms of solving the other side's concerns rather than selling your position. Successful negotiators are solvers, not sellers.

To understand a person, listen to him. Walk in his shoes, or at least try them on. By making the effort to understand someone, we begin to engender trust. Once the other person recognizes our interest in understanding his position, most of the time he begins to trust us, because he senses we are, truly, working to create a solution that will benefit him (as well as us).

Developing trust requires use of all the skills and techniques discussed earlier. Critically important is burying our egotude. Remember that our egotude often surfaces in insidious ways, sometimes unspoken, through facial expressions and other body movements. These movements surreptitiously telegraph our inner, not-so-positive, thoughts to the other person, which weakens the developing bonds of trust, thereby thwarting the ability to reach resolution.

Have you ever been in a conversation about, say, a political issue and recognized the other person's thoughts and outlook clashed with yours? How did you react? Did you turn off your receptors, sometimes right in the middle of the other person's sentence? You didn't allow yourself to hear what the other person was saying, much less listen to it. Instead, your ego developed your response, chomping at the bit, while the other person was still speaking.

This is the insidious effect of egotude. Egotude tells us to believe that what we have to say is more important than what the other person is saying. Egotude dismisses what the speaker is saying so we can start our response as quickly as possible—as soon as the other person takes a breath, even if he hasn't finished his thought.

How often have you failed to allow another to complete a multi-sentence thought? How often have you cut someone off in the middle of his sentence because you couldn't wait to explain why your position was right and what you were hearing was wrong? Think about how you feel when your thoughts are interrupted. Think about how you feel when your sentences are cut off before you finish. It's unpleasant, annoying, irritating, frustrating, insulting, demeaning. It's a lot like being cut off on the road. We have to work to remain—or regain—calm.

Other people feel the same way.

It's all due to egotude. Has egotude ever caused you to feel, as you listen to another, that his comments are so unimportant (and/or wrong and/or irrelevant and/or meaningless) that you are entitled to be rude? Did you cut him off? Why?

Egotude convinced you that your position was so much smarter (or relevant, or meaningful)—in fact, the only right position. Haven't we yet learned there is no such thing as the "only right" position? There is no such thing as universal reality. When you feel that you are about to succumb to egotude, treat it like a disease. Before you are overcome with the need to interrupt, dismiss, or pontificate, take an "anti-ego" pill and make it go away. Patience is a simple antidote. Just remind yourself to be graceful enough to give his thoughts the same respect you want others to give yours. Allow the speaker to finish.

Let me tell you a story. On the first day of my first semester starting my first year of law school, I learned a lesson that, as you will see, I have never forgotten. Most of the students in our class of approximately 150 were milling around before the first class, searching for their assigned seats. Everything seemed so overwhelming, so new. I was nervous. I really didn't pay attention to my surroundings—to the people standing at the front of the lecture hall and speaking with each other.

Unbeknownst to the class, the negligence professor had arranged for an incident to take place among several students in the front of the classroom. A conversation morphed into an argument and then escalated into a pushing and shoving match. I hardly noticed when the individuals who were talking to each other in the front of the classroom started to raise their voices. I was wrapped up in my own thoughts about my first class in law school. A bit more comfortable with my surroundings, I sat down feeling prepared, yet fearful that the professor might call on me to respond to an inscrutable question—one that I might or might not be able to answer. Eventually, I noticed the students in the front of the classroom, but my thoughts kept returning to the fear of the dreaded question that I would not be able to properly answer in front of my classmates. Rather than concern myself with the action in front of me, I focused on my mental preparation for the class that was about to start.

The professor entered the lecture hall. In that split second, the shouting at the front of the class turned into a pushing and shoving match, which was quickly stopped by the professor. From the podium, he asked all of us, as our first exercise, to write down exactly what had occurred at the front of the classroom. We were given five minutes to write what we'd observed. Then we passed our papers down to the first row, where they were handed to the professor. He randomly selected five papers to read aloud.

LISTENING!

None of the five students whose papers were read had observed, heard, or recalled the incident in exactly the same way. The recollections spanned the spectrumfrom a conversation to an actual fight. I was amazed. All of the students were bright individuals who had excelled throughout school, yet each of the five recollections was different. Some of them quite different.

What I learned—and will always remember—is that each person carries with him a filter, based upon the sum of his unique experiences, through which he hears and observes. For example, a person who came up from the streets and saw arguments and violence all the time may have perceived what occurred as merely an everyday minor argument. Yet, another student who lived a cloistered and protected life may have seen what occurred as a brutal attack by one student upon the other. The reality is the facts as we perceive them to be. As the modernist writer, Anaïs Nin, said, "We don't see things as they are, we see them as we are." It is our reality, perhaps quite different from anyone else's. In fact, isn't each person's perception his only reality of the moment?

Perhaps you just finished a tough first day of negotiation. You leave feeling good that much was accomplished and that with another negotiating session or two, you will be able to complete the deal. The next day you call your adversary and find him unavailable. At first, you think nothing of it, but then days pass without a return telephone call. Initially, you rationalize that your adversary is engulfed by another matter or perhaps took a previously scheduled vacation or took ill. But, additional calls and an e-mail or two are met with silence.

In this circumstance there is generally only one rule that prevails: "A deal that is stalling is a deal that is dying." What to do? You must find a way to break the negative inertia of a stalled deal.

What happened? You thought the first meeting was great. What you must do is admit to yourself you are wrong. How do I know? Because you have not even received a return telephone call to say:

- The client killed the deal, or

- We are just too far apart, or

- We needed to finish that first day, or

- I am sorry, I was overwhelmed by such-and-such matter, or

- I am calling for Mr. Jones who asked me to apologize on his behalf for the delay and tell you he'll respond shortly, or

- Whatever.

No. Instead, you have been met with silence. Apparently, despite what you had thought, no mini-relationship was begun. You must accept that, in all likelihood, you said or did something that was perceived as:

- An insult

- A deal killer

- Another negative action

It doesn't matter. Take responsibility.

Maybe you offended your adversary's assistant. Maybe you annoyed your adversary. It's a pretty good bet that you did or said something that was perceived as an insult. The fact that it was doubtless unintentional really doesn't matter. Accept responsibility.

Don't convince yourself you were right and your adversary is a jerk. What does that accomplish other than pat your ego? Acknowledge the reality. Pick up the telephone. Call your adversary. What do you have to lose? Your ego can handle it.

If your adversary won't answer, talk to his secretary or his legal assistant. If you want to rehabilitate the deal, call and talk. Water the barren divide between you and your adversary with conversation and communication. Be humble. Ask questions. Tell him that you are upset because you assume you offended him. Baring your soul often helps. It's okay to show your humanity! It's almost impossible for your adversary not to respond in a positive way. Then probe to uncover the deal-staller so you can divine a deal-saving solution.

What we say and do may not be understood by the other side in the manner that we intended. And vice versa. To confirm a meeting of the minds and assure your understanding of what was said, ask questions that enable the speaker to clarify and confirm his statement, position, or feeling. We all have to work to continually develop our ability to understand.

Most people consider clarifying questions to be a compliment; such questions show your interest and desire to understand. Questions imply your recognition that what the other person has to say is important enough for you to make sure you understand it. It shows your desire to make sure you have it right—that you really "get it." Asking good questions is a plus-plus.

However, understanding becomes impossible if you have a case of rising egotude. Your egotude convinces you that what you have to say is more important, and the elements of your position are more valid, than the other side. As a result, your egotude will impair your ability to listen. It will become virtually impossible to understand the other side. Have you really gained anything by trying to prove yourself right before you understand the other side?

Let's say you are trying to set up a meeting to negotiate a deal, but it is looking impossible to agree on a day to meet. The times they are able to offer are all inconvenient for you. You have a choice on how to proceed.

You can cut them off and say, "There's no point in this—I can only meet you on these days at these hours." Or, you can listen to their available days and hours and their reasons, which may be entirely legitimate. For example, they may need to attend a conference or deal with a series of medical appointments.

The key is to understand that the other side is not deliberately being difficult. Why assume that they are trying to demean you? After all, they are half of this attempt to close a deal. Their stated reason is their incredibly hectic near-term schedule. Can you adjust your schedule without feeling dismissed? Can you work with them to find a mutually acceptable meeting date? Given the situation, it would be gracious to point out that, on certain days, you can make yourself available on short notice. In so doing, the meeting date can be accelerated if the other side has a last-minute cancellation.

By taking the time to understand the reasons for the other side's time crunch, the possibility of a meeting date that is better for you may be created. By understanding the problem, you are able to create additional solutions. The other side will probably go out of its way to call you in the event of a cancellation, because you took the time to understand their needs and concerns. You have created a contingent yes out of a no, not now. A win-win for both sides because you kept your egotude in your pocket and didn't take their schedule issues personally.

Let's consider another example where adversaries start off on the wrong foot. Say you offer an early compliment, which your adversary misperceives as insincere, even demeaning. While you are surprised by the response, the fact is that you didn't really observe and listen, and did not realize the magnitude of the perceived insult.

At times each of us says something without realizing that it was taken the wrong way. Yet, if we paid more careful attention, if we truly listened, we would have recognized the discomfort our remark caused, or we would have sensed a chilling of the conversation. The negotiator who senses a negative response and thinks, "What a fool the other side is being" without understanding why, is perhaps the greater fool. Be the negotiator who picks up on his adversary's discomfort, smothers his egotude with grace, and says to his adversary, "Was there something I said or did that has upset you? If there was, please tell me because I want you to know it wasn't intended." Who do you think is the better negotiator, the more effective spouse, the better parent? Who do you think is the more graceful being?

Good negotiating skills and grace just go together.

We increase our ability to understand by using techniques that show we really want to get it.

PRACTICE POINTS

- Attitude is everything.

- Keep your attitude positive. When it's not, catch yourself and change it back.

- Successful negotiators, parents, etc. seek to solve problems and issues, not sell their preconceived positions or solutions. Be a solver, not a seller.

- Don't allow your egotude to cut someone off. Don't let your egotude allow you to mentally wander off or fixate yourself on your own thoughts and ideas.

- Stay in the now. Listen for the silent end of a sentence. Listen for the pause at the end of a thought.

- Perception is each person's reality. We each live in our own reality.

- Each of us sees the world through our life's prism. We see things not as they truly are, but as who we are.

- NEVER allow your ego to tell you "the other person is naïve or uninformed or what they said or the way they reacted is foolish."

- NEVER assume the other person understands what you have said as you intend it without confirming the other person's understanding.

- NEVER assume you understand what the other person said as they intended, without confirming your understanding with the other person.

Chapter 8

E-MAILS—LURKING MINEFIELDS

LISTENING!

To be a good negotiator, we have to be a good listener.

We must listen and hear with all of our heart, with the desire to understand, not to sell our idea or assert our need to be right. By listening with focus, we hear what the other side is saying. We don't just observe; we really see what they are doing. Careful listening helps us to learn the other person's hidden needs and expectations. More often than not, people disclose more about themselves than they think.

Good listeners use all of their senses, so it follows that the most effective way to negotiate is in person. When we negotiate in person, with concentration and focus, we are able to hear more than just words. By observing body movements, we hear and see the changes in inflection, intonation, cadence, and volume. The full smorgasbord of input, so to speak, offered by our adversary in a face-to-face meeting lets us take in through all of our senses the information we need in order to understand him. We can digest, or synthesize, all of this data so that we become a more effective negotiator.

By this logic, a negotiation via telephone must be less effective, since it leaves all of the work to one sense—hearing. Having lost the valuable input that observation provides in a face-to-face meeting, we must focus extra hard on the conversation. To help focus, try to visualize the person speaking. Of course, it would require a videoconference to observe what the other person is doing while he is speaking. For example, he could be saying to you, "I'll think about it," while he is making a face to his colleague indicating "no way."

Since we can't see the speaker, we need to listen closely to his inflection, intonation, cadence, and volume—the entirety of his aural clues. Because we lose the input we receive in a face-to-face meeting, we need to ask lots of questions in order to make sure we really get what the other side is saying.

In fact, telephone negotiation is less effective, and even more so if the telephone is on speakerphone mode. When conducting a negotiation via telephone, always try to do so without using the speakerphone. If the other person is on speakerphone mode, wait a few minutes and then politely ask if he would pick up the handset. If he resists, tell him either that you are having a bit of a problem hearing all that he is saying, or that you don't want to miss anything he is saying. The speakerphone eliminates the last drop of intimacy, making it difficult even to hear the words spoken on the other side, much less the subtleties of change in tone, intonation, cadence, and volume. Furthermore, it picks up background noise. Also, many speakerphones do not allow the other side, as they are speaking, to hear interruptions. As a result, parties to a conversation via speakerphone could be "talking over each other" with neither realizing the other is speaking.

Now let's examine the least effective way to negotiate or communicate—e-mail. We can only use our eyes in e-mail negotiation. But our eyes only see dry, lifeless, written words. There is no infusion of humanity, via body movement or vocal intonation. With the invention of e-mail, one of the great benefits of the Internet, we have significantly increased productivity. Perhaps the greatest boost to productivity from e-mails is the telescoping of the time needed to set up a meeting. The days of playing telephone tag are gone. E-mails are oftentimes responded to within minutes.

E-mails are useful in many other ways, and can be quite effective in negotiations, too. There are countless circumstances in which e-mail is incredibly effective, but it is a medium rife with opportunities for misunderstanding. An e-mail not understood or misunderstood can be a landmine, delaying and/or even killing a negotiation. Let's see.

LISTENING!

Have you ever received an e-mail that you thought was written with a negative tone? Was it really negative or did you just read it that way? Think about the 150 students who observed the same conversation/ scuffle in my first day of class in law school. Each of them perceived what occurred differently. So, too, with e-mails. Each of us will ingest the words we read, process them through our filter of life, and determine what they mean. That leaves the same sentence at the risk of multiple interpretations. If you want e-mail to be as effective as possible, do not treat it as conversation. Recognize e-mail as a wonderful tool that has increased our productivity. But also recognize its potential to create misunderstanding.

First of all, remember that e-mails never die. They remain retrievable somewhere in the Internet cosmos forever. Not only do they exist forever, it is becoming more and more recognized by our courts that parties have an obligation to maintain e-mails, no matter how many and how old, once it is determined they could be part of the discovery process in a potential litigation. So, not only do e-mails last forever— they may become the subject of mandatory document production in the event the e-mail is related to a litigation. I am not suggesting we need to write our e-mails as if each will end up as evidence in a courtroom, but it just makes good sense to treat our e-mails more as formal letters— not casual conversation.

During the heat of the moment, it's hard to remember that e-mails are written in stone, but we must, particularly since the amount of e-mails most of us receive, coupled with the ever-shortening expected response time, can be overwhelming. As a result, our "completion complex" often takes over. Our completion complex often compels us to respond quickly to complete the circle, to close the loop. We want to clear our inbox for the next wave of incoming e-mails. But if we are not careful, our desire to complete each exchange can result, paradoxically, in a mental sloppiness manifested in the writing of e-mails that could be interpreted in multiple ways. Worse, we may write an e-mail reflective of momentary egotude—an e-mail that should never have been written at all.

Have you ever received an e-mail that has made you upset, even angry, because you felt it was a clear misunderstanding or mischaracterization of what you said? And did you read it as a slight, a snipe? Did you fire back with an e-mail in kind? That's your egotude. Perhaps your e-mails have engendered a similar reaction from others. Therefore, make sure the e-mails you send are clearly written to avoid any misinterpretation.

In this Internet society of immediate response and instantaneous reaction, we often feel compelled to respond immediately, but an immediate response does not need to be measured in nanoseconds. Think about what you want to say before you write it. Think about what the other person has written. Have you understood it correctly (you may never really know)? Hold it and do something else for a few minutes or, better yet, a few hours. Then, reread it carefully before hitting the send key. In fact, some e-mail programs have recognized this need and now are including an Undo option (only effective for a few seconds), just in case you decide, in the instant after you've hit Send, that you were a bit hasty.

The most effective way to write an e-mail is to write it—wait—reread it, and make sure it really says only—and exactly—what you want to say. Reread the e-mail word for word. Don't skim it. Read it carefully! Do the words say exactly what you mean? Can they be interpreted differently? If you are unsure, defer sending the e-mail. Fight your completion complex. Do something else. Wait an hour or so. Then you can approach the e-mail with a clear mind. A clear mind will help ensure that the words you send accurately reflect what you intend to communicate, and will be less likely to be misunderstood. Only then should you grant yourself permission to hit the send key.

It is seldom that I don't edit an e-mail after reading it a second time. Why? I recognize that it could be interpreted differently than I intend. As a result, I always remind myself to make sure that I am writing exactly what I mean: no shortcuts, no skipped words, no cute phrases that could have multiple nuances. Sometimes I hold an e-mail for a day. Sometimes, despite the urge to send it, because it's almost as good as I would like, I nevertheless delete it. Less is usually more. If it doesn't feel really right after a review and edit, it probably should not be sent—ever! I write my e-mails as if I am writing a formal letter, replete with adjectives, prepositional phrases, and qualifiers. I want to make my thoughts as clear as possible so that they will be understood by the other side exactly as I intended.

Always try to write it right. It just takes a little extra effort. And, don't forget—you can always respond in "real time" via telephone.

What if you receive an e-mail that makes you feel demeaned? Why not assume you are reading the e-mail in a way that was not intended? Let it roll off your back. Isn't that the best bulletproof jacket available to protect you from what you perceive to be insulting bullets? It's only our ego that causes us to feel insulted and hurt. How often do we learn that what we thought was offensive was not intended (or if intended, only in a momentary fit of immaturity or anger)?

The best response to a demeaning e-mail is a non-response. At least, no response until it has rolled off your back. Once it has rolled off your back, your inclination to attack will be overcome by your desire to understand. Do so by asking questions in your return e-mail. Questioning trumps answering, whether orally or via e-mail. Asking questions shows the other side that your head is in the deal, that you seek to understand the other side's position, and that you are willing to work hard to find the necessary solutions to make a deal.

Communication quality and understanding deteriorates as the distance between us and our adversaries—from a face-to-face meeting to a phone conversation to e-mail—increases. Only by combining what we hear with what we see can we begin to grasp the full content of the spoken words.

There are those who believe only a small percentage of our understanding comes from words. They believe a much larger percentage of understanding derives from intonation, inflection, timing, and sound level, and a still larger percentage derives from body language. Studies seem to support this belief, as does our common sense. Only in a face-to-face meeting do we hear the words, the intonation, the inflection, and the timing, and see the body language. How else can we really listen with our heart? Hence, an in-person meeting must be the best forum to fully understand the other side. In a telephone conversation, we can only visualize the other person's movements. We can only use our ears to listen to the words and the manner in which they are spoken. We can hear, but it's more difficult to listen and understand, particularly if the telephone call is via speakerphone. Worse yet, e-mails are devoid of any inflection, intonation, cadence, and volume and, of course, devoid of body language. E-mails only allow us to read the written word. Oh, how easy it then becomes to misunderstand or misinterpret!

Let's analyze some basic word groupings. How many ways can they be interpreted? Let's start with the over-used phrase, "See you later." That can mean minutes, hours, days, weeks, or never. But, it's easy to find out what is meant. Just ask questions. To understand what the other side means, just ask, "When would you like to meet again?" or "When would you like to get together?"

Let's take another over-used grouping of words that often come up in a non-business context. Let's analyze the phrase, "I love you." "I love you" spoken by a man on one knee with an engagement ring in his hand is a pretty clear message. Is the message just as clear when "I love you" is uttered at the end of a conversation between friends? What if the friends are of the opposite sex and they used to date? What if they just broke up? Just exactly what does the phrase "I love you" mean in each context? Was it the same as the "I love you" spoken by the man proposing marriage? I think not. What if I used "Luv ya" instead of "I love you" in the examples above? Does anything change? Perceptions are as unique as the human experience of the reader or listener—yet, they are the reader's or listener's reality.

My advice: never assume that what you intend will have been fully conveyed as you intend via e-mail unless:

LISTENING!

- You have reread the e-mail while in a neutral frame of mind.

- You have reread each word, phrase, and sentence to be sure it reflects exactly what you mean and intend.

- You have slowly reread what you are writing to ensure it truly reflects your overall point and the overall tone you wish to convey.

In more instances than we might recognize or wish to admit, our words do not accurately reflect our thoughts. None of us are that good. Yet, we take e-mails for granted. We treat them too much like casual, spoken words. That would be okay if the recipient were directly in front of us, seeing and hearing and absorbing the totality of our words and feelings. However, e-mails are far from that. Be warned—e-mails may be hazardous to your communication and interpersonal health. By taking the extra time to set aside and later reread, and rewrite if necessary, the e-mail, we might be surprised to find ourselves changing the entire message of the e-mail—turning it from a negative into a positive, from creating or exacerbating a problem into finding a solution. Best yet, from a "nasty-gram" into a dealmaker's letter.

Is the BlackBerry sometimes a poisonous fruit? It just used to be a summer fruit.

PRACTICE POINTS

- Good listening requires us to use all of our senses.

- In person conversations allow us to absorb all the input available from the speaker:
  — Words
  — Intonation
  — Cadence
  — Inflection
  — Body Language

- In person conversation creates the best chance for full comprehension.

- Telephone conversations remove the input of body language —significantly reducing the chance for full comprehension.

- E-mails remove sight and sound. E-mails reduce communication solely to dry, lifeless words. How difficult does it then become to understand what the writer intended. It's best to keep e-mails to facts and "time, date, and place" information. If you have more to say, why not call.

- Are you "hiding" behind your e-mail, at least some of the time?

- Before sending an e-mail, stop and think. Can it be misperceived or misinterpreted? Is it 100% clear? Is it devoid of multiple interpretations? Are there unintended nuances?

- Without feedback, can we ever be completely certain an e-mail will be understood exactly as we intend? Consider a telephone call.

Chapter 9

THE CROSSWORD PUZZLE OF LIFE

It is clear to me that, although I started writing about becoming a better or more effective negotiator, this is really a book identifying guideposts to a more effective life, techniques for becoming a more effective person by conducting ourselves with positive attitude and grace in any circumstance involving another person.

Of course, I am writing about both negotiating and becoming a more effective person, perhaps even more so about the latter. If we see all of our interactions as a sort of negotiation, then we can bring positive attitude and grace to every encounter. What a win-win for both parties!

It's easy to interact well with people who agree with us. This book is intended to help us more effectively interact with those who are not in sync with us, who are not on the exact same page as we are. Even people on the same side, whether a spouse, colleague, or other team member, may perceive differently the path to a common goal. Hence, even in a non-adversarial situation, negotiation is necessary to bring two or more people ("the team") into harmony—to move forward in a uniform and cohesive manner—thereby enhancing the team's efficacy and chances of success in reaching its goals. On any day, your team may be your children early in the morning discussing plans for the weekend, your colleague during the day as you formulate a strategy for a particular project, your dry cleaner after work as you seek a quicker return of your clothing, or your spouse over dinner as you discuss what movie you want to watch later that evening.

Several years ago I attended the second day of Rosh Hashanah services—the religious services celebrating the Jewish New Year—in Florida. Normally, I would attend services in the northeast at my regular temple, but because my mother and brother are "first day only" Rosh Hashanah observers, I do not attend services the second day when I am in Florida with them, which had been my habit for several years.

For some reason, not yet entirely revealed to me, several years ago I decided to attend Rosh Hashanah services in Florida on the second day, by myself. As always, I found the service peaceful and grounding as I reflected on the past year and strove to be a kinder, gentler, better person in the coming year. However, my second day attendance was especially rewarding because of the Rabbi's sermon. I found Rabbi Pinsky's sermon so fascinating that I incorporated portions of it into presentations of my own. I would like to share some of those reflections with you since they very much relate to what we've been discussing.

Rabbi Pinsky's sermon—it was about crossword puzzles—compelled me to work on the puzzle in Continental's in-flight magazine. I spent several hours working on a difficult puzzle in the Continental magazine as I traveled to Los Angeles to give a speech, but also had the chance to recall and reflect on the Rabbi's teachings that second day of Rosh Hashanah.

When I was younger, I would try to complete the crossword puzzles in *The New York Times*. I found that I was rather proficient in the beginning of the week, but less so as the week wore on. I eventually realized that the difficulty of the puzzles graduated from easiest on Monday to the most challenging on Sunday—the famous "killer"— *The New York Times Magazine* crossword puzzle.

What, you're wondering, could possibly be the connection between crossword puzzles and becoming a better negotiator or crossword puzzles and enhancing your effectiveness in life? I would like to share several of the more important ones with you.

The first principle—the first connection—is the most fundamental. The more you work on solving crossword puzzles—the more practice you get—the better you will become at solving them. The improvement is simply a function of experience.

Why do we get better at doing puzzles the more we do them? One reason is that many clues recur. So, too, do other persons in negotiations— adversaries or colleagues—demonstrate similar needs, desires, and concerns. Details will vary depending upon specific circumstances, but the similarities constitute the basic psychological and emotional traits of Everyman. Similarly, certain types of negotiations include the same basic substantive issues. For example, when negotiating the sale of goods, the timing of delivery, method of payment, and opportunity to inspect the goods for defects will likely arise. These issues recur in virtually any context involving the sale and delivery of goods. Also, the more we work on solving a puzzle, the more we understand the editor's mindset. In virtually all contexts, as we understand the other side better—friend, colleague, loved one, or adversary—the easier it becomes to find solutions.

Second, when working on a crossword puzzle, it's best to do so without distraction. So, too, in a negotiation, it's best to initially prepare alone. That allows us the chance to free-think the issues that we expect to be raised in order to analyze and internalize them, and then create measured responses and counteroffers to each deal point. Perhaps the best preparation for any meeting or negotiation is the silent time. We need to allow ourselves, our Self, the opportunity to analyze and understand the issues and the potential solutions, not only from our own perspective but also from the perspective of the other person, even if the other person is a member of our team, or an adversary who, for any reason, is on our side with respect to a particular point.

Third, and contrary to the prior point, sometimes it's best to work with others when doing a crossword puzzle. From time to time, I might ask my seatmate if I could interrupt to obtain his help with a clue I simply couldn't figure out. More often than not, together we quickly solve multiple clues I couldn't solve by myself. There are times when working with others is quite helpful in solving a puzzle.

So, too, it is often valuable to bounce an idea, a solution, a problem off someone else in order to obtain feedback and, perhaps, a different approach. Too often, our egotude prevents us from seeking such help. When you are acting as an advisor, whether a business manager, accountant, lawyer or other type of consultant, it is always best to spend some time brainstorming with someone, particularly with your client. Doing so will enable you to share your free-thought ideas and draw out your client's true needs, concerns, and desires. It will enable you to begin to fill your quiver with arrows of solutions to use in the negotiation. In other words, discussions with your client-team member will cause you to better understand the issues that are really important to your client, as well as those that are of less significance. By so doing, you become better prepared to make the trade-offs that may be necessary to reach an agreement with the other side.

Fourth, many tools are available to you when you work on a crossword puzzle. It is not a sin to use them. It is not fattening and you certainly will not be breaking any law. Your dictionary and thesaurus are welcome friends—as is the Internet—as you grasp for a good definition of a word or for a synonym for an answer that seems to be right but does not fit. A colleague can be invaluable as a source of insight or a sounding board—perhaps to provide a different perspective. Seeking help from others—a colleague or Gerhardt the mechanic or the young clerk behind the return desk at a department store or a stranger from whom you are seeking directions is, by the very act itself, a compliment to the one you believe can help you. What a wonderful way to elicit the best from another as you recognize their ability to help.

Fifth—and one of the most delightful aspects of working on crossword puzzles—comes when I take a break and then pick it up again and figure out an answer that eluded me. These breakthroughs feel like epiphanies, the surge of delight that comes from finally getting it. On a subconscious level, you think about and overcome the difficulties that were embedded in the question. The best part is that these breakthroughs seem to always come at the most unexpected times—often, after I put the puzzle down and returned to it, sometimes hours later. The time lapse provided me the opportunity to clear my mind and approach the clue with a fresh perspective. This thought process is known as intuition.

LISTENING!

Although the word is often used today to mean a conclusion not based on rational thought, in fact, it means grasping knowledge without conscious reasoning. The Latin root of the word means to contemplate.

We have already discussed the benefit of a fresh perspective in connection with e-mails. Reread them (always—not some of the time) before sending them. Likewise, I have come to understand that in negotiations, by finding the opportunity to reflect on a meeting or a conversation, an approach or answer may appear, as if I am able to finally understand the problem, really see it. Once I understand the problem, a solution is almost always close at hand. With a time-out, I can often realize or perceive something I didn't realize or perceive before. Perhaps I recognize the true meaning of a phrase or word repeated by the other side. Perhaps I finally see the hidden clues and make the connections between comments and responses when I take the time to reflect on the totality of the conversation or negotiation. Only then do I understand the other side's motivations and concerns.

Sixth, it is fascinating how words without any relationship other than as answers in the puzzle eventually intersect and connect in order to provide a piece of the solution to the entire puzzle. So, too, might we find things people say in seemingly unrelated and unconnected contexts providing a connectivity that will lead to an understanding of what they are really saying—what they really mean. A casual conversation over coffee with the other side's attorney prior to going to the negotiation may very well provide tidbits of information that, when linked with the attorney's or client's comments at the meeting, might connect and help you to better understand their motivation. Perhaps the attorney might have made an offhand comment about difficult times in his client's industry. Yet, when combined with a subsequent negative comment by his client, the meaning of his client's comment may take on greater significance. These seemingly unrelated comments may interconnect to offer clues to what the attorney is really trying to protect, preserve, or obtain on behalf of his client.

Seventh, in order to solve a crossword puzzle one must delve into the clues. Many clues contain intentional misdirection. For example, I struggled to find the answer to "city southeast of Rome." It was a five-letter answer. I visualized the map of Italy but simply couldn't think of any five-letter cities southeast of the capital. Of course, I should have thought of point 4 and consulted an atlas, but it was unavailable to me during the plane ride. I tell this story in my speeches sometimes.

I ask the audience, "What is a five-letter word for a city southeast of Rome?"

The answers range from five-letter cities in southeast Italy to five-letter cities in Africa and the Middle East. However, my frame of reference did not allow me to think beyond the territorial boundaries of Italy. It's interesting that I was unable to mentally cross the Mediterranean and think about cities in North Africa and the Middle East. I had developed answers to other clues to the point where the answer contained the letters T, C, and A; yet, I remained baffled. That is, until I put the puzzle down.

Upon returning to the puzzle, I had a partial breakthrough. I allowed myself to realize that it might not be Rome, Italy, at all, but Rome, New York. Once I allowed myself to recognize that there were many Romes, and already having three letters of the city, T, C, and A, I eventually realized it was Utica, New York. My frame of reference was limited to my own experiences in travel and seldom do I travel in upstate New York. I travel internationally more frequently than I travel to upstate New York. In fact, I haven't traveled to upstate New York for several decades. It was easy for my frame of reference to limit my horizon and focus me in the wrong direction—Rome, Italy—as opposed to Rome, New York, or any other city named Rome. Was it because I visited Italy several times and had fond memories, particularly of when I was visiting my daughter during her college semester abroad?

Now, it's not relevant whether the editor made this clue intentionally deceptive or not. All that is relevant is that my frame of reference—my experience, my perception—led me in the wrong direction. I struggled because I didn't understand the question. I misperceived it. I thought the question was referring to a city southeast of Rome, Italy. But that was not the question. Not the direction of the puzzle editor. My frame of reference automatically added the (wrong) country. On the other hand, perhaps someone living in Albany or Syracuse, New York, would have immediately thought of Rome, New York.

So, too, in negotiations, how often might we misinterpret what is being said—and insert the wrong country, so to speak? How often might the other side (intentionally or unintentionally) misdirect us? How often does our ego allow us to take for granted that we understand what the other person is saying? So much so, that we sometimes even stop listening before we hear everything that is being said. It's so hard to understand a clue, or another person. We have to always focus and use all of our heart and all of our might. We need to ask questions and listen carefully. The next time you lose your focus or drift away from what someone is saying, perhaps this little story about a city southeast of Rome will remind you how hard you need to work to understand what is really meant (the clue) by the other person.

Eighth, the beauty of being a crossword puzzler is that you are constantly given new beginnings—new challenges. This is equally true in taking on a new deal and in new encounters in everyday life. Perhaps it's a negotiation to resolve what you and your spouse will do Saturday afternoon. Maybe it's about what movie you will see that night, or what clothing you will wear to an upcoming event. If the last such conversation was a bit heated, here's your chance to do better. Most of life's encounters are, to a greater or lesser extent, a negotiation with our friends, colleagues, and loved ones (not an opponent or adversary)—friendly, pleasant, and comfortable because of the repetition, but nevertheless a negotiation.

Ninth, there is always an easy way out. In the Continental Airlines inflight crossword puzzle, the answers will be found several pages behind. But the easy way deprives us of the satisfaction of self-completion. In fact, do you find that the more you look at the answers, the more hollow the satisfaction of completing the puzzle?

So, too, in deals. We have the option of fighting for the positions we know our employer or our client wants, or not fighting quite as hard as we should. Some advisors simply go through deal points and accept virtually whatever response they receive, perhaps because of inexperience, fear of being yelled at, or any number of psychological reasons sapping their ability to cope with confrontation. However, when we give in or get less than is reasonably "gettable," the satisfaction level drops. Oh, yes, the deal gets done and perhaps the client or employer is satisfied. Yet, deep inside, if we know we could have done better without killing or delaying the deal, we lose some of the fulfillment. We only reach fulfillment when we can tell our inner self that we did the best possible job under the circumstances—anything less than that reduces the psychic fulfillment points our inner self awards us.

Tenth, in crossword puzzles, those who work with a pen do not allow themselves the luxury of being human—of using a pencil and an eraser to correct mistakes. Crossword puzzles remind us that making mistakes is okay. Leaving them uncorrected is not. The elegance of a crossword puzzle is that it allows you to make mistakes, correct them, and achieve full credit for a completed puzzle. Furthermore, when you work a crossword puzzle in ink, you might tend to hesitate to fill in answers because you fear the self-imposed consequences of being wrong. But by using pencil, you give yourself the gift of changing your mind as you learn something new.

The same is true in negotiations and in life. We are bound to make mistakes. We are bound to inadvertently and/or unintentionally offend the other side. We are bound to misspeak. None of these mistakes are, in and of themselves, horrible. They are simply mistakes—not horrible at all. What makes mistakes horrible is our allowing the mistakes to remain uncorrected. Perhaps because our egotude does not allow us to correct them.

So, for example, say you utter something that unintentionally offends the other side. How do you know? You observed his reaction. He raised his eyebrows, opened his eyes wide and pulled his entire body back a bit.

LISTENING!

Why would it be inappropriate when you see such a reaction to comment, "I hope what I said to you was not taken the wrong way—it certainly was not my intention to offend you"? Are you so important—are you so controlled by your ego, are you so perfect—that you are incapable of acknowledging that you made a mistake? Perhaps unintentional, but a mistake nevertheless unless your ego convinces you to foolishly disregard the other person's reaction. Haven't you experienced another person wincing or squirming or otherwise reacting negatively to what you said? Perhaps it surprised you. Ask questions. Don't allow that reaction to remain without being neutralized. The simple recognition that you have somehow made the other side uncomfortable—even if you were correct in saying what you said—should nevertheless not prevent you from inquiring about the other person's discomfort.

Oh sure, there are times when you must say something that will be uncomfortable to the other side. When you are forced to give an absolute no to a request, it may make them uncomfortable, but that's not the kind of discomfort I mean. I am referring to discomfort coming from a careless remark—intentional or not—perceived as derision or scorn. Our use of demeaning words or movements is the cause of insidious festering in our adversary that can delay and even kill deals.

A straightforward no will never kill a deal if it's said in a non-arrogant way. There are many ways to say no when the only possible response is no. You can preface the no with "I'm sorry but I have no choice but to say no" and then offer a credible answer, such as, "It's company policy" or, "You're too young" or, "I'm too tired, honey." Of course, the more plausible the answer, the easier it is to accept the no by the other side. The simplest "because" is generally better than none at all, if said sincerely. "No—I am sorry, it's company policy" is a pretty lame excuse even though it might be true. Yet, even that is better than a flat-out no. A flat-out no may be perceived as curt or otherwise harsh, not because you intended it to be harsh, but because you might have been somewhat uncomfortable in saying no so it came out sounding brusque. If you must respond with no, make it a gentle no—devoid of egotude.

Having learned the "Ten Connections" between crosswords and life, perhaps the next time you work on a crossword puzzle, you will stop a moment and compare your approach to the puzzle with and how you deal with the interpersonal elements of your life—particularly the negotiated interactions with others.

Most things intersect at some level. Intersections can create "ah-ha" moments.

PRACTICE POINTS

- Practice doesn't make perfect, but it moves you in that direction.

- Focus is key.

- Don't allow your ego to prevent asking for help.

- Use all tools available to succeed, whether a dictionary or a colleague.

- Allow yourself to reflect. Reflection begets epiphanies. With reflection, seemingly unrelated actions and comments are seen in an overall context that can be quite revealing.

- Often, the questions divulge the questioner's direction and perspective. Sometimes the answers are hidden in the questions.

- Every day and every encounter is a chance for a new beginning. Start fresh. There are no strike-outs in life.

- Don't be afraid to err. Successful people make mistakes. They are successful because they adjust and fix them. Successful people do not disregard mistakes, or, worse, conceal them.

- Mistakes are a learning experience.

Chapter 10

EVERY DAY IS A NEGOTIATION

O ften implied and sometimes expressed throughout the preceding chapters, in one way or another we participate in a negotiation virtually every day of our life. For example, how might an eighth-grade teenage girl, let's call her Joanne, approach obtaining a curfew extension from her mother? Joanne is a very nice young girl who does well in school. She would like to persuade her mother to extend her curfew on weekday nights from 8:00 PM until 9:00 PM. Let's walk Joanne through this process.

Now, Joanne, your first idea might be to try the direct approach. You could simply approach your mom and ask for the curfew extension. But Joanne, I don't recommend that you do that. If you do, you will most likely receive a no disguised in one of the following responses (probably in question form because your mother loves you, you are a good student and a good daughter, and your mother doesn't want to respond with an outright no):

- Why do you need it extended?

- What's so important that you can't be home by 8:00 PM?

- Don't you think you are too young?

- Don't you realize how dangerous the world has become?

As you can see, Joanne, your mother's reaction is likely to be a disguised no in the form of a multiple question response. So what I want you to do, Joanne, is to preempt that response. Having read this book, Joanne, you know that once you receive a no, it's hard to convert it to a yes. Even though most no's are not final, the no that you will likely receive, Joanne, will be at least a "time-delay" or conditional, let-me-think-about-it no. It may not ripen into a yes for weeks or longer. So, rather than allow the other side—the adversary, your loving mother—to invest herself in a preliminary no (in this case, implied by a response with multiple questions), instead try to understand what your mother is concerned about. Why not prepare? There are two basic ways of preparing for this all-important negotiation.

The first approach is to think about how you would feel and react if you were in the other person's shoes. Joanne, how would you feel if you were in your mother's position? As a mother, what concerns would you have? The second approach is the opposite: just think through what you want and why you need it—or think you deserve it—and make the request, hoping your mother takes the time to fully respond.

I suggest that you avoid the "It's all about Joanne" approach. Do both. You don't want your mother to simply respond with a flat no, or "No, you are too young." Those two responses sound like deal-breakers to me, and, Joanne, you certainly don't want to set yourself up for a deal-breaker response in what is hopefully only the first inning of the negotiation.

Instead, Joanne, after you think through your needs and wants (your "side"), think about your mother's needs and concerns (the "other side"). What is it that she will need from you in order to feel comfortable enough to give you a yes? To figure it out, free-think the deal and try, Joanne, to understand your mother's position. What is your mother's perception? Make sure you overcome your egotude. Your ego may be telling you that you are old enough, wise enough, mature enough, and deserving enough to expect your mother to simply agree. That self-perception is irrelevant. It is only your mother's perception that counts. But to understand your mom, you must first put your egotude in your pocket. Divorce yourself from your perception. Then, you can think about what your mother might be thinking about and perceiving.

First, you must recognize that the world is a dangerous place. So assuming your mother believes you are a responsible person, she is correct to consider the risk of potential exposures—pedophiles, false friends, drugs—which you have not experienced, and do not have the ability to handle safely.

Let's start with how you should craft the negotiation to give you, Joanne, the best opportunity to obtain either an immediate yes or a "soft no" that might soon turn into a yes.

What do you need to present to your mother so that she will be comfortable with a curfew extension? Now, you may think that you shouldn't even have to ask for an extension. Your mother should know you are old enough and experienced enough to deserve it. Your mother should trust you.

Incorrect thinking! Remove your egotude. Try to see it from your mother's perspective. Perhaps it's not so much a matter of trust as it is a matter of parental concern: her fear of the unknown, the fear that she will be convinced against her judgment to allow you more latitude than you were ready to handle, and both of you having to pay the consequences. These are legitimate parental concerns. Even though they may not be expressed by your mother, she feels them. Sometimes her anxiety may express itself in ways that are not so pleasant to hear, but her concerns are still legitimate. If you wish to win her over, Joanne, you must acknowledge that.

To succeed in this negotiation will require more than words— withmost parents, words alone just won't cut it. In fact, in life words seldom cut it. It's actions that count! Make sure that you are meeting the "action preconditions" to obtain a yes. Have you performed your side of the deal? For example, are you coming home within the current curfew? If, for any reason, you are going to be late, even by just a few minutes, do you call your mother so that she doesn't have to worry? You may, in reality, only be a few minutes late, but without that phone call—which is responsible and is simply common courtesy—that wait for your safe arrival can seem like hours to parents. Prevent your mother's anxiety, so that it does not fester and grow out of proportion and result in an immediate hard, immovable no.

Have you considered using the "salami" approach? In other words, rather than seek an extension from 8:00 to 9:00, could you live with an initial extension from 8:00 to 8:30? Then, spend a few weeks with an 8:30 curfew in order to give your mother a comfort level. Show her that you will meet your new responsibility. These actions speak far louder than promises and casual reassurances. Likewise, the actions of an individual or a company over time reflect the true essence of who the person is and what the company stands for, regardless of their words.

Or are you sophisticated enough, Joanne, that you feel comfortable negotiating for a 9:00 curfew, fully intending to settle for 8:30 after a little back and forth between you and your mother? If you plan to use that approach, make sure your initial request will not be taken by your mother as so outlandish (say, midnight) that your mother cuts off the negotiation before you can play out your moves to reach the compromise you knew you would be happy to accept.

Perhaps, as most teenagers, you don't feel there is enough time in life to spend going through the salami approach. You really want—need, can't live without—the curfew extension to 9:00. Okay, then you need to explain (negotiate) your way to what you want. What does your mother want to hear you say and believe you mean when you say it?

First, she will want to hear you speaking maturely and comfortably, with an understanding that you are aware of the risks of staying out later, and that you will take (at least) the same precautions you are taking with the 8:00 curfew. Remember, it is not that your mother wishes to deny you the privilege of staying out later, although 9:00 may be too late for a school night; rather, it is your mother's fear of what could happen and how she would feel if anything bad were to happen to you.

The only way for you to overcome that fear is to convince your mother that you are old enough, mature enough, responsible enough, able enough to remain in control of your surroundings to protect yourself during the curfew extension. Now, you might still get a no.

LISTENING!

Your mother may feel that 9:00 is simply too late for a school night. So, as you freethink your position, you must initially decide if you will request an extension to 8:30 or 9:00. That's a decision—a strategic decision—that you need to make up front. Do you negotiate for 9:00, or do you seek a shorter curfew extension? It's the same with a request for an increase in your allowance. Do you seek $75, willing to settle for an increase to $50, or do you "open" with $50?

Your instincts know what time (and what amount) you should request. They'll give you the right answer if you don't confuse your instincts with your egotude. Rely on your instincts and common sense, your understanding of your mother and your understanding of the entire dynamic surrounding kids your age. Too much to think about? No, it's not, Joanne—that's why it's called preparation. But one thing is for sure, Joanne, if you negotiate with your mother with an understanding of her fears, needs, and concerns, this otherwise emotionally charged negotiation will be less likely to turn into a conflict.

Now remember, your mother may respond in one of several ways. Once again, think through in advance the responses she may make. She may get angry. She may act shocked. She may act in a demeaning manner towards you. Regardless of her reaction, do not respond with your egotude. If your mother treats you like a little girl, let your anger pass. It may simply be her difficulty in recognizing that you are growing up. Don't be angry at her for that. Simply explain that your friends are getting approval (if it's true), and you simply want to share the additional homework time and socialization time with them. If you think through your mom's potential responses in advance, you will be mentally and psychologically ready to respond without injecting your ego into the situation. Then, even if you end up with a no, it will most likely only be a short-lived no. Your mother will eventually recognize that the way in which you handled yourself shows that you are, indeed, growing up, and that you are becoming responsible, all of which may very well allow her, at least from time to time, if not permanently, to provide a curfew extension to 9:00.

Another example. Let's assume this book is purchased by an executive trainee, Andrew. Let's explore how Andrew might go about seeking a raise from his boss. Andrew has been thinking about how he should approach this incredibly important event with his boss.

In many respects there is very little difference between Joanne's preparation strategy and what Andrew should or will do prior to meeting with his boss. Similar to Joanne, if Andrew is to obtain the best result, he must think through in advance what he wishes to tell his boss and what may motivate his boss to give him a good salary increase. There are many ways to approach this all-important negotiation, but no matter which approach he uses, Andrew should individualize his presentation to make it easier for his boss to justify an increase. By individualizing the presentation as much as possible, Andrew avoids the pitfall of comparison—that's a deep pit with sharp edges, because Andrew cannot do all tasks as well as, or better than, all of his colleagues. Only egotude would allow him to think so, but Andrew's egotude is in check.

Therefore, Andrew will set out to present in a clear, concise manner the benchmarks of his productivity and growth during the past year. For example, Andrew would certainly point out the deals he has done but more important, how he added value to those deals. In so doing, Andrew can imply, without saying it, that he is an asset. Clearly, recounting the deals he has done—the business accomplishments—is a good start, but Andrew must focus on his out-of-the-ordinary, if not extraordinary, results. One device to present his great results without appearing to brag is to compliment a coworker, perhaps his immediate superior, from whom he learned the technique he used to obtain an excellent result. By sharing the success, Andrew creates a double positive, one for his accomplishment, the other for his humility. As Shakespeare said, "The aroma of the rose lingers on the hand that casts it."

Value-added enhancements to the organization will set Andrew apart, but they are not easy to relate while remaining both sincere and humble. Body language, voice tone, and eye contact play a critical role in appearing sincere and humble when we talk about ourselves.

LISTENING!

Therefore, in order to be comfortable, Andrew should practice talking about his accomplishments out loud, preferably watching himself in front of a mirror. Many of us are uncomfortable complimenting ourselves. Practice will allow us to do so in a sincere yet humble way, without acting self-disparaging.

Not only should Andrew seek to point out the most notable of value-enhancing deals or the most notable elements of his job performance, but he should also point out his value enhancement in non-substantive areas. He may be participating on committees within the company. He may have assumed a mentoring role, a big-brother responsibility to others. It doesn't matter if his superior asked him to take on the role or if it was his own idea. Without bragging, it will be obvious that mentoring is a recognition by others of the importance of Andrew's feedback and opinion, whether it is with respect to their business issues or, perhaps, personal matters. These actions will reflect well on Andrew's maturity, growth, and leadership skills and his potential to bring further enhanced value to the organization. Last, Andrew must also focus on his personal growth. Perhaps he's assumed more responsibility in a religious or civic organization or now spends three days a year helping the homeless. These outside activities also reflect upon Andrew's maturation and growth. Such growth is as important as his growth and enhanced value to his profit-generating potential.

After Andrew has fully prepared, he should request a meeting, and since his boss controls the timing, he must be ready to present his case if his boss says, "Let's do it right now."

Now, Andrew, when you walk into the boss's office, consider saying nothing. Allow the meeting to start with silence—much more on silence later. On the other hand, and depending upon how well you know your boss, you may wish to speak first. You both know the reason you are there. The question then becomes how to start. There are many ways.

An easy opener is to say, "Thank you for taking the time to meet with me. I know you are very busy. I'd like to briefly present to you my credentials for a salary increase." This is simple and direct. It shows strength of purpose. You may or may not be interrupted. Your boss may pre-empt you and say, "There is very little money to go around," "The organization lost money this year," "The organization is under a belt-tightening program at the current time," or any other comment to reduce your expectations or even terminate the meeting. Do not be dissuaded, no matter what your boss says. You must explain that you want to present your credentials for a salary increase whether or not an increase is currently feasible. You want to share how you have grown as an employee and as an individual, so that when salary increases are considered, your boss will have an understanding of why you are entitled to a significant increase. This approach will, at least, get you a good hearing.

Remember, Andrew, your meeting creates the opportunity to paint a verbal portrait of yourself. The presentation of your credentials for a raise or promotion can be almost as important as the successes constituting your credentials. This is your opportunity to create a mosaic that integrates all of your assets. Regardless of the immediate outcome (over which you may have no control), you seek a high grade from your boss. Your entire performance counts. It's not Olympic figure skating—the best and the worst scores are not discarded. To be successful in your presentation, just like star athletes, you must seek to do your best and most important, finish strong, even after a slip, fall, or fumble. Stay in the batter's box, keep taking judicious but powerful swings. No matter what, don't bench yourself.

Let's consider what could be the worst possible beginning. Your boss starts the meeting by recounting a failed deal or lost sales opportunity for which he holds you responsible. How will you respond to this opener? Did you prepare for this scenario? Will you remain silent and hope your boss moves to another area of your performance? Will you disregard his comment and move to a different area of your performance? Will you explain why the failure was not your fault?

Of course not! These responses are all either passively or actively evasive. How should you respond? Address your boss's negative comment directly. You knew the comment was possible, and you prepared for the possibility.

You should say, "I've thought about the failed deal, and I've reflected on what I could have done better to save the deal. As I thought through the transaction, I realized I should have been more diligent in my follow-up. I should have followed up more often as I began to realize the other side was becoming less responsive and probed more effectively into why the other side was delaying. I should not have allowed myself to rationalize the legitimacy of the delay. I should have learned that once a deal begins to stall, like an airplane it becomes more likely to crash. I realize now that I should have been more proactive, asked more questions to learn what was really going on during the delay. I've learned from that experience. I made several errors that cost the company the deal. I won't let it happen again. In fact, I believe that painful experience taught me a great deal, and it helped me to close the other deals I'd like to briefly discuss with you today."

No matter how your boss reacts, this response shows honesty, character, and strength. Good luck, Andrew.

Now, let's consider an entirely different type of meeting. The time has come when you, the boss, must fire one of your hires. In almost every instance, this employee being fired will, in one way or another, negotiate to keep his job. The approach can range from the use of heartstrings to implied legal action. You know he will not want to simply listen and leave, and if he does, he will most likely return after he overcomes the initial shock and regains his composure. You won't escape the confrontation. There are no fixes for this difficult meeting. It is virtually impossible for negative feelings not to surface.

Nevertheless, with compassion and a willingness to share the responsibility, share the loss, the encounter may not be as unpleasant as you expect. The technique of approaching the conversation acknowledging that you, the boss, are partially responsible for what is happening shows compassion and grace. It's also most likely true!

Aren't almost all firings, at least in some part, a management failure? Perhaps the job description changed and your hire's skills were no longer a fit. Perhaps you initially misjudged his skills, or misunderstood his talents and experience. By taking responsibility for what you acknowledge was at least partially your mistake, the sting of failure is lessened. You are your hire's direct superior. Allow yourself to accept partial responsibility for the failure. This approach is generally effective because each of you must share the responsibility. No matter what, be compassionate and keep your egotude in your pocket. Your hire will no doubt test it. Even though he will be leaving, this is an important negotiation. Whatever the relationship was between the two of you, why kill it forever, or worse, make a committed enemy. Prepare and then deliver the message firmly but kindly.

Whether we want to choose the restaurant or the movie, the discussion is a negotiation.

PRACTICE POINTS

- Preparation is key, but knowing "your side—your position" is seldom enough. Think through the other side's perspective and position.

- When asking for something, whether a curfew extension, salary increase, or promotion, think through the following:

  — How can I make it easier to obtain a "yes"?
  — What concerns will the other side have?
  — What questions and surprises will potentially be forthcoming?
  — How do I control my egotude and respond with grace and maturity to the most seemingly embarrassing, or seemingly foolish, questions and the most seemingly demeaning responses. Anticipate attacks on your ego. Disregard them, whether or not intended.

- Prepare, prepare, prepare—look at both sides—and keep the ego buried.

Chapter 11

NEGOTIATING AWAY THE FEARS

LISTENING!

Learning concepts and principles to become a better negotiator is not enough. This chapter will focus on overcoming our negotiating fears.

A brief anecdote: When I was a young attorney, I had to drive about an hour to attend a negotiation that was going to take place at another attorney's office. The other attorney was a very well-known and successful lawyer many years my senior. While I was driving—I remember it as if it were yesterday—the palms of my hands began to perspire. Then, I began scratching my neck, unable to satisfy a constant itch just beneath the collar of my shirt. Perhaps my dry cleaner had used too much starch.

As I drove to my destination, I became increasingly anxious. I knew with certainty that the itchy neck indicated anxiety, and probably the sweaty palms did, too. It was psychological; I needed to overcome some fear.

"What am I afraid of?" I repeated to myself, out loud. "What is making me anxious?" I repeated these questions until the answer dawned on me: I was afraid of the unknown. I was simply afraid of the other attorney. He was older than I and much more experienced. He might embarrass me, I thought, in front of my client!

Once I had zeroed in on the source of my anxiety, I said to myself, "Just do it! You are prepared—just allow yourself to do the best job you can do." Just do it. I wish I thought back then to sell that phrase to Nike! Little by little, I was able to calm myself. The itch on my neck and the sweaty palms soon disappeared.

As it turned out, that thought process was the basis of my preparation.

It was both psychological and substantive. True preparation! I spent the balance of the car ride thinking about what I was going to say, how the other attorney might reply, and what my responses, in turn, would be. I considered the other side's potential moves and tested them against my potential responses, much the way a chess player contemplates the board from both his side and his opponent's point of view. The more I reflected, the more I was able, through this mental preparation, to internalize the issues. My confidence rose and I became comfortable with what I needed to accomplish. I knew there would be times in the meeting when I might be forced to say "I can't agree" or "I don't understand," but I had prepared myself to be able to say them, if needed, without undue discomfort and without ego, and with a follow-up move in mind.

The deal went well. Preparation and internalization are critical to successful negotiations.

It's a good idea to analyze the deal points and rank their relative importance. By doing this, you will be able to trade some points for others. Sometimes there are few actual deal points, in which case you may have to literally create them. By developing a thorough understanding of the deal, you can bring issues into play that could be relevant, but about which your client does not care.

For example, in a deal involving installment payments, there may be an issue of creditworthiness. While your client has told you that he will accept, say, the buyer's signature for the balance due, you might nevertheless ask for a third-party guaranty. Perhaps also a letter of credit. By introducing the concepts of a guaranty and a letter of credit, you have introduced deal points that don't really exist. In so doing, you have created potential giveaways simply by thinking through the deal and realizing it is reasonable to request a guaranty or letter of credit, even though your client does not expect it.

Now, let's discuss confrontation. Negotiations always involve confrontation. The only issue is at what level and for how long. Few of us enjoy confrontation. It's much more fun, and easier, to say yes than to say no. However, confrontation can be a wonderful device to create tension and improve your leverage. You might introduce additional deal points that you may not need to obtain and initially fight hard for each one. Confrontation, properly created, exerts a gentle pressure that often leads to getting more of a yes than would otherwise be the case.

Remember, if you don't ask for something, it's unlikely it will be offered. Simply requesting something does create a sense of confrontation, but do not be afraid to ask if you can justify the request. Remember, even a firm no may eventually soften into a yes, either for the point you requested or a different one.

The key to becoming a better negotiator is to act like a better person. How? By developing your ability to concern yourself with the needs, wants, and desires of someone other than yourself. By becoming more sensitive to others, you will become a better negotiator. By listening—hearing with your heart.

As soon as you realize you are not perfect (Oh, come on! Admit it!), you can start to work to like yourself more, accept yourself more. That is when you become more real. Easier said than done, but "getting real" is a journey worth taking. Now you can better accept the foibles of others and allow their trespasses to roll off. Don't let your egotude get in the way. Everyone came to the meeting to do the deal. Perhaps some are having a bad day or a bad week or a bad month. Perhaps they will be surly or disdainful. Ignore the trespasses so you can better listen to and understand the needs of others and more effectively work to create a solution.

Remember, we are all trespassed upon more often than we like. Yet, it's only a smudge on our exterior. It's never an injury to our heart or our essence. If you think of a trespass as someone stepping on your shoes and leaving a scuff mark, you know that a good shoeshine will make your shoes look new again. An insult is only a dirt mark or scuff on your outside. It will vanish as soon as you take your psychological shower and let the insult wash off your back. Most of all, no one can trespass on your heart. Your essence is safe from harm. In fact, the only person who looks small is the trespasser.

"No one can make you feel inferior without your consent," remarked Eleanor Roosevelt, first lady of the FDR White House. Without your participation, no one can make a fool of you no matter what they say, no matter what they do. You are the only person who can make a fool of you—by what you say or what you do. So, when you find yourself being attacked by your adversary, do not drop to that level. Do not respond in kind. Use a soft voice to disarm the screamer. Take the high road. Don't allow anyone to edge goodness out of you, even for a moment.

Consider another approach to win the moment (and perhaps much more). Consider silence. In the silence that follows the other's outburst, the foolishness of that outburst, not the words themselves, reverberates in the room and in the heads of everyone present.

Silence can be more effective than any other response. Consider the use of silence in calm situations, too. After a question is posed or a response made, silence can be the catalyst for a revelation. If your adversary feels awkward and uncomfortable in the ensuing silence, it is probably because he perceives it to reflect his weakness. Don't say a word! This is the moment when that person will start to speak—to alleviate his own discomfort—and what pours forth may be a revelation. Good journalists know that the best interviews often come when they lead their subjects to leap into a gap of silence.

Since childhood, we have all been told that silence is golden. Since inflation has increased the value of gold, why not use it more often? Use it to underscore a point you just made, to question a point another has just made, to show respect for a point just made, or to jiggle loose a telling add-on comment.

Silence has many uses, many voices. It can be as piercing as a cannon blast, or it can whisper, "Tell me everything."

Silence is a miracle concept. You can compliment someone by simply not speaking. For example, how often have you said something you thought was very important, yet, as soon as you stopped speaking, the other person immediately began to talk about an entirely different or contrary point or just jumped on your point to add his own thoughts? How did you feel? What did you think? I'll bet you felt the other person had dismissed what you said as unimportant, or that he wasn't even listening. You must have felt a bit insulted. You are right! You know you are right because you have done it to others. You have done it when you thought what they were saying was boring, irrelevant, or trivial. You have done it when you thought what you had to say was much more important. We intuitively understand that if another responds a nanosecond after we stop speaking, the other person probably didn't hear what we said, at least not all of it. Our thought processes operate at a multiple of our hearing absorption. Instead of listening, our brains are either filling in the blanks, or getting ready to make the next move, already developing our next sentence. Hence, the noise in our mind drowns out what the other is saying. What is worse, the speaker probably realizes it. Far from a compliment!

So listen for the punctuation at the end of the speaker's last sentence. Allow silence to reign for two or three seconds. Then respond. In so doing, you telegraph to the other person that what they said was important enough for you to reflect on it for a few moments before responding—a clear compliment to the person who has just finished speaking. If you cut off his last words in your rush to take your turn and make your point, it will have the opposite effect.

Let's assume you are the boss and your employee has just finished a report lasting 3–4 minutes. Let's further assume you did not find the information and ideas presented to be of value. Yet, something your employee said triggered a new idea. How will you respond? Will you telegraph you are dismissing the report by immediately moving to the idea just triggered in your mind? Will you probe the report to make sure you extracted everything of use to you? Will you remain silent for a few seconds as you ponder the report, regardless of whether you felt it was worthwhile? What do you think will resonate best with your employee? How will you direct the conversation to your new idea without appearing to dismiss or otherwise demean the report?

Good leaders instill a sense of value and partnership in their employees. Great leaders take the next step and also drill out all the information buried within the employee in order to analyze the situation with all the available facts. Poor leaders cut off and demean (intentionally or unintentionally) their employees. By doing so, they leave themselves vulnerable to a leadership failure. I refer to that failure as the why-didn't-you-tell-me-that syndrome.

"Why didn't you tell me that?" There are few worse questions for a leader to express. It represents after-the-fact failure—when information, if known in time, could have prevented a bad situation or enhanced a neutral or positive one.

Every encounter is a negotiation, even when it's with our subordinate and we have all the leverage.

All of us have fearful thoughts some of the time.

PRACTICE POINTS

- Fear of the unknown spawns fear of rejection, fear of embarrassment, and fear of failure.

- Preparation and analysis trumps fear and lessens anxiety.

- Free think any upcoming encounter. Practice internalizing your statements and potential responses to the other side. Work hard to put yourself in the other person's position.

- Preparation by free thinking both sides, all positions, and internalizing the dialogue can only make us more effective (in any interpersonal encounter).

- Good journalists know that the best interviews often come when they create a gap of silence which the interviewee tries to fill.

LISTENING!

- Use silence to elicit more. Use silence as a compliment. It's a form of ad lib, too. Silence is golden.

Chapter 12

SEVEN MILES HIGH
BUT ONLY INCHES AWAY

Most of us readily divulge too much in response to questions, especially when we are the subject. And especially when we fly.

After my seatmate and I engage in the typical superficial chat, the conversation often intensifies. Usually, my seatmate will respond to my questions, divulging both personal and business information. Sometimes, I can offer insights into my seatmate's most personal issues and problems, and I find myself offering advice and suggestions that would otherwise be considered intrusive or inappropriate. The conversation simply lent itself to probing. Of course, the conversation could not have developed if not for the initial pleasantries. In those very first minutes, my seatmate and I either begin to develop a connection and become more focused, or we turn away and resume what we were doing.

I often ask myself, "Why do so many people open themselves up to personal conversation during an airplane ride?" Let's take a closer look, because several aspects of a good "seatmate relationship" seem to arise in every successful interaction, from a conversation to a negotiation.

Perhaps foremost, the personal space between airplane seatmates is virtually non-existent. Seats in coach are only separated by an armrest, and a rather flimsy one at that. Depending upon our seated position, we might find our legs or arms touching from time to time. In fact, some of us have more physical contact on an airplane ride than on a second date. Due to space constraints, just the physical act of seating oneself often requires interaction. This physical closeness eliminates even the pretense of normal boundaries between seatmates.

The closeness is magnified by the mutual recognition that seatmates are about to share an experience. All airplane travelers share similar concerns and a mutual interest—whether we will have a pleasant trip and arrive at our destination on time. Adversaries in a deal share similar goals: to get the deal done in a reasonably pleasant and uncomplicated manner.

The shared experience often deepens if passengers are required to wait while seated on the plane, either at the gate or on the tarmac. The delay ends only upon receipt of clearance furnished by the unknown, unseen hand of air traffic control who, whether due to traffic volume, weather, or other reasons, determined in the first place the delay over which we have no control. And so, we wait. Together. Until we receive air traffic control clearance. Then, a collective sense of relief, even pleasure, lifts us as the delay ends and the airborne portion of the flight commences.

Concerns of delay, physical closeness, and the typical inconveniences—restroom visits or during the food and beverage service (who doesn't worry about being spilled on?)—all nudge us toward a fledgling relationship. Many of us may be flying for reasons other than pleasure. Some are traveling to address a problematic business issue or emotionally difficult personal issue. Hence, some are traveling under increased stress, regardless of their enjoyment or fear of flying.

In addition to the dynamic between seatmates, consider another element: the flight attendant and his interaction with the passengers. Flight attendants, just like judges and adversaries, are people too. Even though they are professionals, they too bring to their job the everyday concerns and issues in their personal lives. The question is whether, in a difficult situation, they will rise above their personal problems. Will they exhibit grace? How often have we seen flight attendants acting supercilious or dealing poorly with a passenger who is uncomfortable or unhappy, regardless of the reasons? After all, it's easy to respond to pleasant requests. But how will the flight attendant respond to the inappropriate request? The real test, the test of life for all of us, is the manner in which the flight attendant (read: "us") reacts and responds to the difficult passenger.

First, the flight attendant must recognize that many of the passengers are flying for less than pleasant reasons. Perhaps some are visiting a sick relative. Even worse, they may be flying to attend a funeral. Perhaps the passenger is afraid of flying or worried about making a connecting flight. But there are also the high-maintenance types—the passenger who inappropriately feels entitled to a better seat or to a special meal (that he neglected to pre-order), the passenger who cannot accept he is only one of about 160 passengers or who cannot endure the wailing of an infant suffering from the pressurization of the cabin.

The sad reality is that when the flight attendant does not respond well, everybody loses. The problem passenger remains unsatisfied. Other passengers may be disturbed, or may even feel at-risk. Ironically, the big loser may be the flight attendant. Did he spoil his day by failing to take the extra moment to rise above the inappropriate request or tone of the passenger? Refuse the request with grace if it cannot be accommodated. Is it any surprise that the flight attendants who exhibit kindness (grace) in these situations seem happier? Just by being understanding, even if unable to fix things, both the passenger and the flight attendant achieve some sense of satisfaction. An attempt to make things better, even if not possible—as opposed to entrenching ourselves in our "rightness"— often brings a smile. Oh, what a wonderful aphrodisiac kindness can be.

These moments of interaction in the confines of an aircraft, whether positive or negative, are deserving of reflection. Think of the flight attendant as you. The unhappy passenger is your adversary. Maybe he's your garage mechanic, Gerhardt (who has control of the time slot for repair of your car), or your mom (who has the ability to extend your curfew), or your boss (who is in a position to accommodate your salary request). What do they bring to the negotiation? Are they uncomfortable, fearful, perhaps upset about their child or spouse or sick relative? You may never find out. But, why assume their agitation, unhappiness, or curtness is directed at you? It's about them. So keep your egotude in your pocket. Look for the extra pillow or blanket. Exhibit kindness. It's a no-lose approach.

Those who attempt to accommodate the other (sometimes an empathetic smile does the job), notwithstanding their own concerns, will always obtain some psychic fulfillment. A sincere smile automatically extinguishes our egotude. Focus on committing simple acts of kindness. It's that easy. On the other hand, those who feel trespassed upon (by another's perceived inappropriate action or inaction) find themselves needing to see the other person as "lesser" than they. As a result, they "bury their grace" in their need to be right. They bury their grace in their desire to use their control or sense of superiority. Yet, the very vitriol emitted is "backsplashed" onto them. The nastiness that spews forth reflects back in the agitation of self-justification. Then, it reverberates in the widening hollowness of the self-justification.

How many times, after losing your temper or acting superciliously, did you need to explain your actions to others (really to yourself!) to justify what you said or did. Yet, there was no legitimate justification— just a rationalization. Resolve to be kinder next time. Take two "kindness-catch your breath pills." You don't need to go to the doctor for a prescription—you have them. You will quickly restore your grace.

If it's so much nicer to be nice, why do we all too often fail to be nice, as nice as we are capable of being, as nice as we would like to be? Perhaps, it's momentary distress over a trespass, a trespass that has yet to roll off our backs. Perhaps it's a concern we have yet to solve or even entirely recognize, churning up our insecurities and fears. Those insecurities and fears block the gates to the reservoir of our goodness and kindness. When those gates are closed, goodness and kindness cannot flow. We cannot taste the joy of giving. So, keep your goodness gates open. Allow goodness and kindness to bubble up and flow onto others. Then, enjoy the backsplash of your goodness and kindness. Try it, you'll like it.

Let's return to a discussion of the remarkable amount of information seatmates sometimes divulge. Perhaps it's the sharing of an unpleasant flight, similar to employees working an all-nighter. The shared unpleasant experience brings a sense of closeness. So, too, a delayed flight can create a sort of gallows humor. Why? Because we each share the inconvenience and frustration caused by the flight delay, and the frustration of our inability to do anything about it. It produces the camaraderie of Us versus Them.

Once engaged in superficial chat with our seatmate, we decide whether or not to pursue the "relationship." Of course, in a negotiation, the luxury of whether or not to engage does not exist—you must engage. If I develop some interest in my seatmate, it is quite easy to engage with questions that, more often than not, tend to move the conversation into more personal concerns.

Question: Why does this occur? Is it just me or is it anyone?

Answer: Anyone. Anyone who exhibits a sincere interest
in learning about another.

Conversation is facilitated simply because of proximity. We have almost no choice but to look directly at our seatmate as we speak, to focus on our seatmate as he speaks. Moreover, because of the airplane noise, we often need to lean in to hear all that our seatmate is saying. In other words, the circumstances of airplane travel cause us to instinctively follow some of the basic rules of good negotiation. We focus with our eyes and our ears and really listen. It is both the instinctive use of some of the negotiating techniques discussed earlier, plus the togetherness (of the seats), that allows the walls between strangers to so easily break down. With my seatmate recognizing that I am focusing and listening intently, an incipient relationship can easily develop.

But, why is it that someone might open up to a stranger so readily?

Perhaps the biggest, most obvious reason is the assumption that we will never see each other again. Anonymity allows us to more readily share our concerns. Also, our concerns more readily surface from the stress of travel. Stress is the pincer that "squeezes out" the stories. When anything is squeezed too hard, its insides start to ooze out. So, too, when we are "squeezed" by stress, our true feelings and emotions often surface. Questions are pincers, too—just more obvious than stress.

By asking questions of my seatmate, a mini-relationship may develop. Why? Because the questions show my concern, and that concern, when felt, allows my seatmate to begin to trust the sincerity of my interest. Once we sense interest, we tend to open up and share our thoughts (it's no different in a negotiation, is it?).

What seems remarkable is that I can often help my seatmate better understand his issues and problems. But, it's not me. We all can help each other. All we need is a sincere interest. If nothing else, when we open up to another, the verbalization itself generally helps (all of us) to better understand our issues and problems. Is there something special about me? Not at all! All I am doing is listening and hearing with my heart. Seatmate, adversary, colleague, friend, when asked personal questions, most of us want to answer. Most of us love to talk about ourselves. As a result, we are often quite willing to disclose our true feelings. Oftentimes, much more than we realize.

I remember a trip to Seattle in particular. I was sitting next to a fascinating individual who, I would soon learn, was very creative. I was immediately interested. I don't consider myself a creative type, so, when I speak to creative people, I am quite admiring of their ingenuity, their understanding of the most intangible of concepts, and their ability to meld a variety of overarching cultural and communal issues into a clear creative approach, whether through art, architecture, or otherwise.

I had the chance to spend about six hours with my creative seatmate. He was traveling to the West Coast to give a presentation on culture, community, and commerce, and the manner in which they can blend into real estate projects, whether museums, retail stores, or streetscape assemblages. His observations and insights were fascinating. He answered my questions with more and more detailed responses. It was obvious that my seatmate thoroughly enjoyed talking about what he did. He thoroughly enjoyed sharing his perceptions of the confluence of these concepts. The conversation moved forward in fits and starts.

LISTENING!

We were not immune to the various interruptions that occur on a plane ride—announcements, food and beverage breaks, rough patches of air, and the like. Nevertheless, we kept returning to our conversation.

Eventually, the focus turned to my seatmate's company. As he began to discuss the interactions with his partner, I began to hear he was somehow dissatisfied. The basis for his dissatisfaction was unclear, but I could sense a "dis-ease" on his part. So I focused intently on what he said, and listened with all my heart. I listened with all my heart because I was truly interested. Two people sitting next to each other on a plane. One desiring to discuss problems about his partner. The other, me, interested in listening. I had no ulterior motive. I didn't think we could somehow end up working together as attorney-client. It didn't cross my mind. Rather, I was just thoroughly enjoying the conversation. I felt good. I felt I was helping my seatmate draw out his true feelings about his partner and his company. We were both becoming more comfortable. I asked more questions. He continued to open up.

We all love to talk about ourselves. Just say, "Tell me about yourself" and then, sit back and listen. "Tell me" implies our interest. It says, "I want to know more about you." It says, "You have something important to say and I want to listen." To stop whatever else we are doing and focus on them.

The most interesting part of the conversation was the epiphany I experienced near the end of the flight. About thirty minutes before we landed in Seattle, I began to mentally reassemble the words and phrases, as well as his tone of voice and facial movements, when he spoke of his partner. At first, even though I could sense things weren't perfect, I saw no reason to assume anything was seriously wrong. It was natural to assume that my seatmate would simply continue to coexist with his partner (continue the status quo, as most of us tend to do). However, my seatmate was deeply unhappy. My epiphany was that it just wasn't a problem to live with; rather, the status quo was gnawing at my seatmate. So, as we landed and the conversation was winding up, I turned to him and said, "I don't know when it will happen, but I'm sorry to say that I think you may very well 'divorce' your partner." About a year later my seatmate, with whom I had exchanged business cards, called to ask for a meeting. He wanted to discuss dissolution of the relationship with his partner.

Many years after his "business divorce," during a dinner conversation, he reminded me of our first conversation and of the prophetic words I said to him. More interesting, however, were his reflections about our initial conversation. He seemed to marvel at my ability to understand what he was really saying, even though we were complete strangers. I barely remembered the conversation; he remembered it as if it occurred yesterday. It was his life and it very much remained on his mind. He didn't use these words, but he said during our dinner how grateful he was that I had facilitated a thought process that allowed him to open his "unlocked prison door"—the door to the prison of his relationship with his partner. What a big decision! It took almost a year for him to internalize the problem, understand its impact, and actualize (implement) a solution. Nevertheless, he did it. His thanking me for helping him find the strength to move forward in his business life was a well-deserved mutual thank you. He was thanking me, yet he was also thanking himself.

As the dinner progressed, he spoke about my ability to discern his true concerns, rather than simply skate upon the surface issues. As I reflected on that airplane ride, I remembered that I was as much impressed by his failure to discuss the positive aspects of his partnership, as I was with his discussion of the disappointments. Perhaps, because of the pain in facing up to a failed partnership, he, like most of us, danced around, skirted the real concerns. Yet, the bits and pieces he inadvertently disclosed about his partner in the way he spoke (his intonation and facial expressions), and what he did not say (the lack of any positives), allowed me to intersect the inputs. It was like solving a crossword puzzle. As each piece began to intersect, I began to see more clearly. Eventually, I realized there was much more of a problem between him and his partner than he was verbalizing.

LISTENING!

What I did was neither more difficult nor more impressive than what any of us could have done. We just need to focus on the conversation. Show a real interest by asking questions. Then listen with all of our heart and all of our might. Was I taking a chance by asking personal questions? No. My "listening" made it clear to me that my questions, probing as they were, were being taken as sincere attempts to understand and help him solve his problems, and in fact, they were. I was fully immersed in the conversation. Fully sensitized. So much so that I could adjust my questions if I sensed I was going too far. The gratification I received in helping my seatmate crystallize his thoughts and feelings was quite real. What a great flight.

Negotiating with your heart—opening yourself up to others to help them understand themselves—will enable you to create solutions. It may improve your own well-being by improving your self-understanding. You probably have had experiences similar to mine. Perhaps you were waiting on line at the motor vehicle bureau to renew a license, or in a similar less-than-pleasant situation. While you were waiting, you struck up a conversation; started a mini-relationship. Ironically, it is in these unpleasant circumstances that we are most apt to reach out to another person. In so doing, our daily existence becomes enriched just from creating a mini-relationship and trying to understand (help) someone else.

Maybe you say, "Why bother?"

Bother because it will help you become a better negotiator. It will introduce more grace and fulfillment into your life. I promise.

On the other hand, there are times when I am doing the talking rather than the listening; I am sharing my problems or issues with a colleague— even a stranger. At the very least, I get the benefit of verbalizing my thoughts and listening to myself. Was I the "real deal"? Was I speaking with a protective coating of words? Was I really addressing the issues that were concerning me?

When you speak, are you being real? Observe the listener's facial reaction. It's a clue. Do you sound credible, or are you just emitting "background noise"? Are you hiding your true concerns, skirting the real issues?

When I feel enough trust and confidence in another person, I open up even more. By so doing, I allow the listener to help me explore my real concerns. Perhaps make a suggestion or put forth a perspective I hadn't considered. It is surprising how graceful many people become when we impart our trust in them.

The techniques discussed throughout this book will work at the "negotiating table of business" and the "negotiating table of life." They will enable us to enjoy a more fulfilled life. Life is fulfilled as a function of the grace (kindness and goodness) we pour over others and thereby pour over ourselves.

So bring down the walls and open your heart. Not only when you are dealing with an adversary, but also in all of your everyday interactions with others, whether family, friends, or colleagues. If you are going to interact with another, however brief the exchange will be, make it meaningful. Even if it's just for five minutes. Give it your all—your complete focus.

Why not try to live every moment in the present moment? Absorb as much of each moment as possible. Don't allow yourself to become caught in your egotude. Your problems are not the biggest or "baddest" or "worstest" in the world. We all have problems. We all have baggage.

Allow yourself to fully interact with others. Bring forth your heart to negotiate a better deal, to create new relationships, and to deepen existing relationships. In so doing, you will taste the true fruits of a successful life. The sweetness of life is not measured by the size of our wallets, but rather by the depth and breadth of our relationships.

Consider the techniques you use to speak to a fellow airplane passenger. They work.

PRACTICE POINTS

- Airplane rides facilitate several good negotiating—

interpersonal techniques:

— Shared concerns (on-time arrival, smooth air)
— Shared on-board inconveniences
— Physical proximity
— Greater focus in conversations to overcome cabin noise and distractions
— Stress (of flying) can either "open up" your seatmate or "clam him up"

- The basics work in almost any scenario:

  — Ask questions. Use questions to show interest and respect.
  — Focus implies sincere interest.
  — Don't interrupt.
  — Use silence to elicit more information.
  — Reflect, just for a few seconds, on what was just said. What a terrific compliment.
  — When you speak, "listen to the listener," particularly the nonverbal reaction.
  — Focus on the conversation. Live in the NOW, the present.

Chapter 13

THE ART OF AD-LIBBING

LISTENING!

Questions are at the heart of negotiation. Questions allow us to control the direction of a meeting and they focus the direction of the response. When we ask questions, the other person feels we have an interest in what he will say, and in fact, since he is responding to our inquiry, he is correct to feel that way. Our interest enhances our listening, which allows us to better understand the other person's needs, wants, and desires. The better we understand, the more likely we are to solve the other person's problems. Surely we will have a better chance to negotiate a successful resolution.

It is crucial to be able to ask the type of questions that will allow us to better understand the other side. That understanding will help us direct the negotiation toward the points we wish to address and resolve. However, it takes work to determine what questions to ask. It's a key part of the preparation. Negotiations (the conversation) seldom follow any particular direction, or result in addressing any particular deal issues, at least not necessarily in the order we would like.

Therefore, to be a good negotiator, you must also be a good ad-libber. There is no technique to develop skill at ad-libbing, but the ability to think on your feet is important. Negotiators are as good at ad-libbing as their personality allows. Some are better than others. Usually, people who are uncomfortable in their skin, uncomfortable with confrontation, uncomfortable with accepting a no, are often poor ad-libbers. They are less capable of humanizing the interaction or using other techniques to break down the barriers existing between parties. For the negotiator, good ad-libbing is a real plus.

A good negotiator must also be a good actor. He must be able to control the fear, hurt, and other emotions that may be welling up inside, and maintain the composure that will allow a calm response. Never a response out of rage. A response out of rage puts the speaker on the stage of fools. Rage is the display of temper. Rage may cause us to disclose our true sensitivity to a particular point. A response out of rage has a high likelihood of being outrageous. Rage can cause us to say things we wish we hadn't said—express feelings and thoughts we never intended to convey. All we accomplish with rage is a foolhardy disclosure. Worse, a disclosure we may not even realize we communicated.

Do you think you are too in-control ever to give away your secret thoughts? You would never unintentionally disclose anything. Nothing slips out of you!

Think back to arguments you have witnessed when the adversaries spoke in rage. Did they disclose emotions and feelings they wish they hadn't? Have you ever noticed politicians respond to an uncomfortable question? They are well-practiced in spouting the right words, even when caught by surprise. But their true feelings are telegraphed with a tightening of the lips, or a facial tic, or perhaps an awkward body movement. Spend a few minutes on YouTube and you'll see what happens when politicians or pundits respond to hecklers in ways (with slurs) they wish they hadn't. Despite their contrition, we know we have seen a side of them that may be exposed when they are angry and unguarded. In their normal rational life, they are able to neutralize their prejudices. However, when their anger opens the door, their prejudices surface. It may not be who they really are, but only who they may have been in the past (or only a small portion of the totality of who they are today). Yet, they nevertheless earn the stigma of being prejudiced, arrogant, and demeaning.

It is instructional to observe people who are on the world stage as they respond to a question that catches them off guard, embarrasses them, or causes them to feel attacked. In essence, we are always on stage when we are with others. We are on stage with our peers in a conversation about where to have lunch, or with our adversary as we attempt to resolve an issue in our favor. In any of those circumstances, you may be presented with a question you do not fully understand, are not prepared to answer, or will lead into an embarrassing response. How does a good negotiator deal with such questions? How do we avoid the pitfalls of misspeaking? How do we avoid being pushed in an uncomfortable direction, or having to go on the defensive in order to respond to a question? A negotiator must learn when and how to ad-lib, how to parry or diffuse difficult questions.

The best ad-lib is often repetition. Respond to a difficult or unexpected question by asking the questioner to repeat it. "I'm not sure I understand. Can you repeat what you said?" or "Can you be a little clearer?" or "Would you tell me what you meant by that?" all will buy a little time. Furthermore, since people rarely repeat their question word for word, the restating often provides vital clues. Repetition allows the negotiator to catch his breath. Without giving anything away, he can recover from being caught off-guard and/or unable or unwilling to answer the question. Equally important, the negotiator gets a "second bite at the apple." The question, when it is repeated, may be expanded. As we learned from crossword puzzles, many times the answer is hidden in the question. We simply need to understand the question. We need to know if we are talking about Rome, Italy, or Rome, New York, when the questioner asks us about Rome.

There is a subpart to the technique of repetition. Instead of asking for complete repetition, focus on a few words or a phrase and ask for specific clarification. In so doing, it will not appear you don't understand the question at all. You just need clarity with respect to a certain portion. The questioner should sense that you are really trying to understand. As a result, the questioner may divulge a great deal more information as he attempts to explain to you (either in a demeaning or sincere manner—it really doesn't matter) what he was trying to express.

What if the questioner demeans your request for clarity or repetition? So what! If he is demeaning, he may drop his guard. He may allow you to continue to probe, thinking you are not up to his level, not his equal. Take advantage of his sense of superiority, and put it to work for you. Push the questioner to open up in order to help you, the person he perceives to be "the less intelligent, less informed, less whatever" listener.

Try combining either the technique of compliment or self-deprecation with the technique of repetition. "That's a very good question," you might say. "But just so I'm sure I understand exactly what you are asking, would you mind clarifying your point?"

By the same token, as long as you don't overdo it, you can use self-deprecation to put the other side at ease, perhaps causing them to lower their guard. For example, you might indicate that you didn't understand what they were saying. You might say that what they were addressing was an area you really didn't fully understand, and would they further explain their point, their position, their perspective. Their response, any response, will give you additional time to think through what they are saying. They may divulge answers to their questions. They may disclose their positions, all from the manner in which they rephrase the question. All you need do is listen carefully. Listen carefully to the changes in the repetition and the clarifications. It is in the changes and clarifications where clues to hidden compromises and fallback positions may be found, where the true meaning and intent may be glimpsed. Reflect. Allow yourself to recognize and analyze what the changes and clarifications are really saying.

Let's assume the other side continues to ask questions of you. They are controlling the direction of the meeting. Perhaps it's because of something you or your client said—a comment that opens the door and allows the other side to probe a particular area you wanted to avoid.

Let's say that in the midst of a negotiation your colleague mentions that the Acme Company, which recently went bankrupt, is a customer of your organization. A completely innocent comment. Perhaps the bankruptcy was known to many, having been reported in the press. However, the linkage of the bankrupt company to your organization—

the fact that it is a customer—probably was not known. Yet, your colleague, a bit naïve, didn't even realize he mentioned the connection. However, the other side has now assumed that the bankruptcy of the Acme Company, your customer, could have a negative impact on your company's business. As a result, the other side is now given the opportunity to probe the relationship between your company and the heretofore seemingly unrelated bankrupt Acme Company.

This is a line of inquiry you didn't expect and want to stop, and stop quickly. You are now on the defensive. You must explain why the bankruptcy of the Acme Company, one of your customers, will have little or no impact on the profitability of your company. Your adversary starts gently by asking how long you have been doing business with the bankrupt entity. Then, slowly but surely, the questions become more probing. Your adversary seeks the mother lode—the amount of sales (and perhaps profits) between your company and the Acme Company. With that information, the questioner may be able to suggest your company may be in a weakened financial position. He will then be able to seek greater financial assurances from you. What's a good negotiator to do? How can this line of questions be fended off? Perhaps the best evasion is avoidance. It's like taxes. It's legal to avoid them, but woe to those who evade them.

There are several avoidance techniques. At their heart is the ability to quickly and smoothly (can you ad-lib?) change the subject, from an interrogation about the relationship between the two companies, to a subject that is unrelated. It can work when the new topic is more germane to the negotiation. Of course, the simplest technique is to make light of the relationship and quickly move on. But the other side may not let go. In that situation, try offering a half-answer. Indicate you think the relationship is minor but you'll look into it (avoidance by deferral). Then, before you can be questioned further, move to a more germane subject.

You might try to deflect the probe by a self-deprecating joke. In an ad-lib, you might indicate it was you or another colleague who worked so hard to get the Acme Company's business. Now, it's kaput. Laugh it off. Then, joke that perhaps some of your commissions are in jeopardy.

Or, if true, look your interrogator in the eye and simply say, "I don't know anything about the relationship." Don't make small talk about it. Whatever you do, don't engage in speculation about it. Quickly move to another topic.

You also have a bucketful of other avoidance techniques. There are bathroom breaks, lunch breaks and all sorts of call-the-office breaks. If the meeting is at your office, you can use the feigned break of seeing a colleague walk by and making believe you are being summoned. Then, get up, excuse yourself, and say you need to speak with him about something "that's important but will just take a minute." Break the continuity. Diffuse the attack.

Is it illegal, immoral, or fattening to see one of your colleagues pass just outside the conference room and pretend you are being signaled to step out for a moment? You need to create an artificial break. You need to step out of the batter's box and break the rhythm of the other team's pitcher. Of course, in that context, you will need to drag your naïve colleague with you so he cannot be questioned in your absence. Whether it's immoral to feign an emergency to break the questioner's attack, I leave to you. You won't go to jail—it's not illegal, and you won't gain weight—it's not fattening. Sometimes, the situation just calls for a punt. Forget about the "Hail Mary Pass" unless you were the quarterback for Boston College.

Another technique of avoidance is minimizing the issue. Indicate there are many more important deal points to be addressed and resolved, which should be attended to since time is running short.

Nevertheless, let's assume the other side continues to aggressively focus the conversation on the issue of the bankrupt customer. Furthermore, he personalizes his attack. Perhaps he accuses you of being evasive, and otherwise lashes out with attacks on your integrity. He insinuates that your company has a culture of "stonewalling." He may throw other "jabs" to prick your composure. He may want you to respond with anger.

LISTENING!

Do not allow yourself to lose your temper. You must retain your composure. Keep your egotude in your pocket. Take a deep breath. Keep reminding yourself that no matter what you are hearing, it's not really personal. Let it roll off your back. Okay, so you're in an awkward situation. Your company's soft spot has been exposed. Whatever facts you may know, you certainly don't want to disclose anything else— certainly not facts that can be construed negatively.

So what can you do? You can continue to push the conversation to other topics. Continue to minimize the relationship between your company and the Acme Company. Reiterate that it is irrelevant to the negotiations. The Acme Company is only one of many customers. Moreover, if you really don't know, why not punt? Just say, "I don't think we were doing much business with them. I don't think it was very high margin business. I'll check after the meeting, so, for now, let's move on." Then, immediately take control by asking a germane deal-based question, even if you would have preferred to have raised that issue later in the meeting. However, because of the attack in a potentially delicate area, do what you need to do to derail the probe.

All of this mental action happens simultaneously. You can do it. You can determine how to change the topic. You can control your emotions. You can overcome your annoyance with your colleague's naïveté. You can certainly disregard any trespasses upon you by the other side. You must maintain your emotional temperature at 98.6 degrees, while at the same time diffusing the probe. But all of this takes practice, practice, and more practice.

The beauty of practicing to become a better negotiator is that it doesn't require a negotiation. It's just as important to think about the concepts we've discussed. Apply them to prior episodes in your life. How did you handle them? How might you have handled them better by using some of these techniques?

The best politicians and the best performers never allow themselves to lose control, no matter how nasty the heckler. The best of the best diffuse the heckler by ignoring him, by joking, or by using self-deprecation. Only in extreme circumstances should a heckler (or anyone) be attacked. If attacked, the attack should be delivered jokingly. Those who attack the heckler with anger are the losers. They are seen as stooping to the level of the heckler. What worse experience can an audience (your colleagues) have than to witness someone they admire (you) allow himself to be irritated by a heckler and respond in an unseemly or unprofessional way? How often are our friends or colleagues (or adversaries) our hecklers? Isn't the whole world truly our stage?

Perhaps you remember, even now, the epithet hurled at a man by a high-level politician from Virginia. It was made after his speech. At that very moment, months before the election, he lost his bid to become a presidential nominee. It only took one word. One ugly word uttered in a moment of anger. But, all that is irrelevant. What matters is that the senator indicated a prejudice which effectively caused the immediate disintegration of his potential presidential candidacy.

And who doesn't remember the former "Seinfeld" sidekick, Kramer. The actor who had played Kramer similarly lost his temper during a comedy performance. No one remembers or cares about the nature or extent of the heckling. All that is remembered is his outburst and the disappointment of the audience. That response may follow him for the rest of his life. Will it fade from our collective memory?

So, too, things said in a negotiation are remembered. However, what is remembered in negotiations, just like all human interactions, is not the everyday humdrum, the typical back and forth. Rather, what is remembered are the high and low points. The statements that are made, which are incredibly pleasant and deal-supportive, and the statements that are made, which are incredibly nasty or deal-killing.

But what if you are really stuck? You truly don't understand the question or don't feel prepared to respond. Why not quietly and politely say you would prefer to table the inquiry? You'll return to it either in a post-meeting telephone call or at the next meeting. It's never inappropriate to admit lack of knowledge or inability to properly respond to a question. Why not say you would prefer to answer the question when you are in a position to answer it properly? You might say you are deferring the question because you don't want to misstate your company's position.

Whenever you are stuck for an answer to a question, or are caught off guard, use a question to catch your breath. That's the "graduate-level" use of questions. It's a great ad-lib. And you thought you couldn't do it! We are all able to ad-lib. It's easy. Simply ask a clarifying question. This will provide the opportunity to compose ourselves and develop a comfortable, non-aggressive response. Try to develop other "ad-lib" responses. We can spend a lot of time discussing how we can really become a good ad-libber. However, the skill is a function of how comfortable we are in our own skin. This cannot be taught.

There are so many ways to buy time with an ad-lib. Time is relative, at least according to Albert Einstein. It's malleable. You can mold it, stretch it, perhaps even turn it inside out if you own a starship with warp speed capability.

However, if you are uncomfortable at a meeting because you are ill-prepared, prepare better next time. On the other hand, to the extent you are uncomfortable because you feel overwhelmed by the other side or otherwise feel in a lesser position, remember only you can make a fool of yourself. Disregard the other side's trespasses. Do not lose your temper, fake answers or pretend to be someone you are not. Just do as the kids say—just "be real." That's the best way to not make a fool of yourself. It requires putting your egotude in your pocket. Being yourself. Not faking it. When you're stuck, ask questions. Request more explanation. In most circumstances, the other side will recognize your humanity (from your request), and will help. Moreover, their egotude may cause them to take you for granted and under-assume your ability. Take advantage of that circumstance whenever it presents itself. You do not need to show the other side how smart you are, how experienced you are, how much smarter you are. To the contrary, without overdoing the self-deprecation (which can boomerang when overdone),why not allow the other side to feel superior? Oftentimes, they will then divulge too much, or otherwise let their guard down. This dynamic may allow you to obtain more information.

To become a good ad-libber, simply live in your own reality. Just recognize that who you are, what you know, and what you have to say, is just fine. You will be just fine. Just don't fake it. Don't try to be something you are not. By following this advice, you will learn to ad-lib in a way that is comfortable for you. Remember, the more you conduct yourself in your own reality, the better you will become at finding the right thing to say. Even if you commit a faux pas, you will be able to neutralize or overcome it because you will have observed the other side's reaction. Then, after digesting the reaction, you can adjust with a follow-up comment to make sure that they understand that what you said was meant as a well-meaning comment, question, or answer, and not an attack.

Be real.

It's not hard to avoid embarrassment. Only we can embarrass ourselves.

PRACTICE POINTS

There are so many ways to ad-lib.

- We can all ad-lib when stuck for a response:

  — Use repetition. Repeat the question, either entirely or in part.

  — Ask for clarification (either of a part of the question, or the entire question).

  — When the question is repeated, focus on changes in the wording. Changes offer clues.

  — Use silence to draw out the questioner.

  — Never lose your composure. Don't be swallowed by your ego. Statements made in rage are often outrageous.

LISTENING!

— It's not a sin to say, "I don't know, I'll get back to you."

— Whenever stuck for a response, take the question and rephrase it while asking for clarification. Don't be afraid to say "I'm not sure I really understand your question."

Chapter 14

LITTLE THINGS MEAN A LOT

It's the little things that define who we really are. In relationships of any type—formal negotiations or everyday personal interactions—we are defined by the extent to which we conduct our lives with kindness and grace, as opposed to negative characteristics spawned from egotude.

For example, Thomas Alva Edison is admired as the father of the incandescent electric light bulb, and then, so that people would be able to use his invention, he developed a method of generating and distributing electricity. Historians might describe him as an industrialist and a successful businessman credited with 1,093 patents. Is that how we define him? Perhaps—but that is not how Mr. Edison is wholly defined. Like all of us, he is truly defined by the way in which he dealt with others. He was, indeed, a genius who steadfastly continued his experiments until he succeeded. But Nicola Tesla and George Westinghouse would surely add that he treated them unfairly, even ruthlessly. You decide.

How do you define yourself? Are you the person who excels at what you do at all costs, without regard to the feelings of others? Or, are you the person who works to find solutions and does so, to the greatest extent possible, with kindness and a desire to do the right thing? It truly is the little things that count. How many of us ever break the big rules? How many of us break any of the Ten Commandments that would land us in jail (the others are just as important)? Conversely, how often do we find ourselves not treating others the way in which we would like to be treated? How many of us always, "Do unto others as we would like them to do unto us"?

These departures from grace occur all the time, often in the simplest and most unwitting forms. Perhaps the one most difficult to control is the judgmental response. How often do we listen to our children, our peers, or others, and react dismissively? How often does our face, our voice, or our words express all too clearly disdain, disappointment, or disapproval? When we respond judgmentally, we take a step away from reaching a rapport with the other side. Forget about gaining their trust! When we respond judgmentally, we distance ourselves from our true objective: a relationship with the other person, to solve their problems so we can reach consensus. We all recognize the negativity (and wrongness) of judging someone else. Isn't that a job best left to a higher authority? Furthermore, when we judge others, we are somehow acknowledging our own flaws and insecurities. After all, it is easy to point out someone else's imperfections—we recognize them in ourselves!

However, we can learn to control our judgmental responses. We simply need to listen to the other person with our heart and recognize that what they have to say has value. Their statement is a verbalization of their perceptions and feelings at that moment. We may not agree with their perceptions, and we may not understand their feelings, but perceptions and feelings are subjective. When we are busy thinking that our opinion is more important, intelligent, or incisive than theirs, all we hear is the white noise of our own judgment. If we listen without judgment, we can silence the self-satisfying interference of egotude and begin to understand how that person arrived at his position.

Once we find the source of their perceptions and feelings, we can work to change their position. Attempting to understand others' perceptions and feelings is an expression of respect for them. Understanding can only develop if we allow ourselves to accept what another has said as being worthwhile, regardless of what was said and what we think of it. When we remove our need to judge, we remove the egotude spawned by our need to feel superior. We no longer need to believe that what the other person has to say is inappropriate, unimportant or irrelevant. Now we can listen with all of our might and all of our heart.

LISTENING!

If we attack or dismiss someone else's opinion, how can we expect others to listen to and understand what we are saying? When we speak to prove we are more right or more relevant, we are talking at the other person, not with them. To gain the other side's trust, we must telegraph that we are listening so that we can understand what they are saying. If we can gain their trust, it will put them at ease to tell us more about their perceptions and their positions. If we show that we respect them, they will help us to understand them.

Sometimes, the best way to get what others are saying is to reflect the feelings they are exhibiting. In other words, reach out and touch the other side with empathy and/or sympathy. It's an effective way to really understand the emotions and perceptions attached to another's statement. For example, if the other side makes a statement with pathos, or another non-negative emotion, "catch" that emotion. Allow it to reflect back onto the speaker. Perhaps you might say, "I understand it's difficult for you to say what you have just said, and I appreciate your saying it." By listening carefully, we can mirror the emotions being expressed. In so doing, the speaker will sense we understand his feelings—his pain, his delight, or whatever emotion is infused into his statement. Perhaps the other side is not exhibiting emotion. He is stone-faced. Nevertheless, the emotions and feelings may be implied in his statement by his choice of words, or his delivery, his tone.

As human beings, we may be unique in our experiences, but we are remarkably alike in our feelings and reactions. When you speak, especially about something important to you, aren't you more comfortable when the tone of the listener's response reflects your emotion? Don't you feel better if you sense that they "get" it? Of course you do, and so do I.

In your follow-up question, or in the manner in which you ask the question, reflect the other person's emotions and feelings. It's another effective way to reach out with empathy to that other person. After you speak, don't you feel more comfortable when the listener's response (question) shows he is trying to fully understand what you were saying?

What if the other side responds with apparent belligerence? What if your adversary asks, "How can you take that position?" or "How can you say that"? We can allow ourselves to be offended. On the other hand, we can recognize that, implied within those words, may be surprise, disappointment, perhaps even shock. By allowing ourselves to be sensitive to the underlying emotions and by choosing to assume the best, we can then better respond.

How one handles the little things constitutes advanced negotiating techniques. It is often the little things that define (and disclose!) who we are. We certainly cannot consider ourselves kind and graceful individuals if we judge everyone else's statements and actions. On the other hand, if we see the other person as our neighbor, we will react and interact in the very same manner we would want them to react and interact with us.

There are many techniques available to draw out the other side, to enable us to better understand their perceptions and positions, so we can find solutions to their problems. Sometimes, as already discussed, silence can be an effective tool. People tend to become uncomfortable with silence. Try using silence after the other person finishes speaking. Control the urge to immediately respond. As a result, the speaker may assume you did not understand what he was saying. He may take it upon himself to elucidate further. Silence can act as a "poultice." Just as that native tribe in the movie "Congo" surely had balms and salves to draw out infection from a wound, so, too, silence can draw out hidden festerings and underlying concerns. Silence can be particularly effective when we are not entirely certain what the other side was saying.

Of course, we can always probe with questions, but in some circumstances probing questions may seem too intrusive. In that case, try silence, coupled with a direct focus on the person who just spoke. Oftentimes, this will produce the desired result—a clarifying statement.

Another tool that can be quite effective to draw out your adversary is intentional self-disclosure, divulging something that might otherwise be deemed private or personal. For example, if someone is telling us about his business problems, we might respond by disclosing we have similar or analogous problems. It's similar to two airplane travelers sharing their concerns, allowing the parties to recognize the humanity of each other.

Such a responsive self-disclosure may break down the wall between the parties. Both parties may begin to understand that not only are they in the room with the same goal—to do the deal—but also they are experiencing similar business or personal issues. Humanizing the interaction often enhances the understanding of the need to work together to find solutions. When that happens, impasses tend to dissolve. Remember, negotiators are both there to do the deal.

How do you determine when to make personal disclosures, when to use silence, when to probe with questions, and when to use the other techniques described throughout this book? There are no hard and fast rules. No lights will go off and no signposts will appear. Rather, each of us needs to operate in the present moment. Each of us must use all of our might and all of our heart to listen to the other side. In so doing, our instincts will tell us when to apply each of the techniques we have learned.

Another technique to draw out the other side is the use of the premature yes or the premature no. Prematurity is most effective when discussing a point you are prepared to concede. Offering an early yes to a point that you know full well you will concede later may be seen by the other side as a reason to believe you will be reasonable throughout the negotiation. It may reduce the other side's urge to play hardball with respect to all of the points it is prepared to concede.

The opposite technique—the premature no—can be equally effective. However, unlike the premature yes, the premature no is a bluff. You might offer a premature no so that a conciliatory yes offered later in the negotiation has more impact. These techniques (the premature yes or premature no) must be employed more with instinct than design. Of course, you must first be well prepared so you will understand which issues you will concede and which you will not.

Mutuality is so obvious it almost need not be addressed, but I would be remiss not to mention it. By virtue of the parties meeting to negotiate an agreement, they have the same goal—to get the deal done. In essence, both parties are there for the same reason. Why not suggest "communal brainstorming" to resolve some of the most difficult points? Mutuality suggests that you put the issue on the table early and say, "Let's throw this around and see if, together, we can find a solution that can work for both of us." For example, assume all of the parties know full well there is one issue that could create an impasse. It is an issue for which neither party has so far been able to find a solution. This approach shows a willingness to listen to all sides and all views. It evidences an implicit willingness to compromise in order to solve the impasse.

Be able to recognize when a particular issue cannot readily be resolved. On the other hand, the fact that an issue cannot be resolved by 11:41 AM does not mean it will not be "resolve-able" at 4:51 PM. By the end of a day of negotiations, this knotty issue—and other unresolved issues that have surfaced over the course of the day—when combined with the interpersonal glue that (hopefully) has developed, may then resolve as compromises emerge to reach agreement.

Just as a no is usually only a "no, not now," so, too, an impasse with respect to a particular issue does not mean it will remain an impasse forever. An impasse now can be compromised and solved later if the parties work together to understand each other's needs.

What if one of the parties loses his composure, acts judgmentally, or otherwise exhibits an emotion that is detrimental to the negotiations. Remember, don't personalize the negotiations—it's just business. Generally, we are only dealing with the resolution of commercial differences. Issues in a commercial context rarely involve a challenge to anyone's integrity or character. It's our egotude that confuses the issues at hand with our integrity or character. Usually what we perceive as a trespass is simply due to misperception and misunderstanding. If the impasse focuses on something you said, don't assume you are being labeled a liar. Instead, consider the possibility that the other side misheard you or is misinterpreting what you said.

Many chapters back I promised to revisit hyperbole. Recall the hyperbole used to convince Gerhardt, the garage mechanic, to give you an earlier and more convenient date for automobile maintenance. As you will recall, the hyperbole—perhaps it was a lie—was the story of an upcoming vacation via automobile; it was important that the car undergo a complete tune-up before the trip. The statement was, at best, an exaggeration and, at worst, a lie. Either way a problem.

Hyperbole or lie, however we choose to describe it, we are verbalizing a circumstance which is not a part of our reality. Most of us intuitively understand the insidious self-erosion caused by lying—no matter how "white" the lie. Lying distorts reality. The more we remove ourselves from reality, the more dysfunction we are injecting into our healthy functioning beings. Once we create a false reality, it becomes easier to do it again. We start to live in a dual world: one reflective of the actual reality of the world; the other, reflective of the false reality we have created. This can only cause a "rip in our soul" reparable only by undoing the lie. As we begin to live more and more in the non-real, we move further away from the goodness and kindness that is the reality for which we all strive, whether to exhibit toward others or ourselves. Slowly but surely, no matter how innocent we think the lie or the hyperbole, we prevent the rip in our soul from healing. We begin to define ourselves in the inconsistent duality of the simultaneous real and non-real.

Perhaps this can best be expressed in the jargon of the day. "Keep it real," we hear all around us. This simple expression is perhaps filled with as much philosophical and emotional depth as anything written by the great philosophers. The fact that we hear it from hip-hop artists or our teenage children does not make it any less significant as a guidepost for the conduct of our life. Oh, yes, we may win the moment by use of hyperbole or deception or misleading words. But at what cost? The erosion of our integrity and character—way too high a price to pay, no matter how sweet the moment.

And so, this chapter ends with a simultaneous urging (to be honest) and admonition (not to lie or exaggerate). It is the little things that count. The little things define who we are—the seemingly innocuous little things that we might disregard or lie about. Yet, the little things are our spiritual and emotional glue, the glue that connects the building blocks of who we are—our essential self that we alone are "souly" constructing as we seek to create a life of fulfillment, self-respect, and grace.

WE ALL GET THE BIG THINGS RIGHT. Our true "measure" is often found in how we handle the less significant moments in our everyday life. Are we as kind and graceful in the less important, even insignificant, encounters during our day?

PRACTICE POINTS

- Don't judge. That's for a higher authority.

- Avoid judgmental responses.

- Work harder to understand "where others are coming from."

- Consider brainstorming for solutions to difficult issues.

- Don't personalize negotiations.

- Keep it real. Be honest.

- Integrity and character always count.

Chapter 15

HOW YOU THINK IS EVERYTHING

Physicists are searching for a grand unified theory—also known as the "theory of everything"—to explain, in one elegant rule, how the physical world works. How can we capture and distill all that we've learned here in a single concept? A concept not only enhancing one's negotiating skills, but also enhancing one's journey through life—a concept by which to live.

As a subscriber to *Investors Business Daily*, a daily business newspaper, I find myself gravitating toward a regular feature titled "IBD's Ten Secrets to Success." One of the ten "secrets" is always set forth at the start of the column: "How you THINK is everything." I thought about all the books, articles, and speeches by so many people recounting their success stories—how they made it, and I realized that the bedrock principle permeating those works is, indeed, the way we think.

In Dr. Norman Vincent Peale's seminal work, *The Power of Positive Thinking*, or any of myriad subsequent works, in virtually every context the principle of "the way we think" is the fulcrum for improving ourselves, and thereby improving our lives. In fact, the concepts and techniques addressed in the previous chapters are all subsumed by this concept. Yet, how do we actualize the concept of positive thinking, as opposed to just agreeing with it? How do we go beyond internalization; how do we actualize the power? How do we incorporate positivity (kindness and grace) into our everyday lives? It's easy to reflect on the concept of positive thinking and resolve to become better human beings. How do we use it to help us become more successful in every aspect of life, rather than just a better negotiator?

A policeman stops our car and opens the conversation with the usual, "Driver's license, insurance, and registration, please." How do we conduct ourselves in this situation? How do we maintain a positive mental attitude? Or in the more everyday circumstances—talking to Gerhardt, the garage mechanic, the clerk working the exchange counter at a department store—how do we infuse ourselves, and the situations, with positive mental energy to help us become more successful as human beings?

It's easy. Reflect upon any of the concepts and techniques discussed earlier. Then, apply that concept or technique to the issue at hand in a positive way. Visualize the other side (or yourself) saying yes instead of no. Think in terms of working to obtain a yes. Stop saying, "I'll try," and start saying "I can" or "I will." Delete the words "I'll try" from your life. Those two words allow us to accept the expectation of failure. Make positivity your predominant thought. To paraphrase Henry David Thoreau, what we think is who we are. The more we think about something, the more likely it is that we will eventually verbalize it; and as we verbalize our thought processes, the more likely we will act upon the verbalization of what we were thinking. Mr. Thoreau surely believed we are truly what we think. Our thoughts become our acts and deeds—our thoughts are who we are.

We are what—and how—we think.

The little secret to achieve positive thinking is to do it by doing it. We use positive thinking by thinking positively. Visualize the goal. Shine a different light on it. Play new background music. Rewrite the script. Change clothes. If we think of our attitude as an outfit in our closet that we can wear or change at any given moment, we can think of our thought processes as reflecting who we are at any given moment. Our thoughts are what we are wearing at any given moment. By thinking positively, by neutralizing our egotude, and by lifting the stain from our tie or blouse, we can more effectively negotiate our way through life.

LISTENING!

Let's apply this lofty concept to two different situations. Let's take, for example, an interaction that is scheduled in advance versus one that is suddenly thrust upon us. In either instance, to be successful in the negotiation we need to think positively. We need to think in terms of solving the problem being presented in the most effective manner possible. To be an effective solver, we must disassociate ourselves from our egotude surrounding the situation. A scheduled negotiation gives us some preparation time. We know it's coming. Maybe it's with our adversary, colleague, or employer. On the other hand, when an interaction is thrust upon us, when we are confronted, we do not have the opportunity to prepare. For example, being stopped by a police officer for a traffic violation is a "negotiation" thrust upon us, one in which many of us will attempt to talk our way out of the ticket.

As we hear the siren and see the flashing lights quickly approaching from the rear, our egotude might try to convince us that we were not speeding. Perhaps, as we notice other speeding motorists not being stopped by the police officer, our egotude makes us feel we are being singled out. In such circumstances, our egotude blinds us from seeing the other side, the officer's perspective. Our egotude will prevent us from clearly thinking through the problem, thereby reducing our chance of finding a viable solution. So, let's take off the egotude and think this through.

When we do, our visions, our dreams, enable us to see beyond our next step. They enable us to take leaps in our lives, some small and some quantum. We just need to put aside our rational thought, to open our minds and believe in ourselves. Our visions will stimulate us if we let them. If we let them, they will create mental excitement that will permeate our mind and body. The electrons in our atoms will jump to a higher energy state and our mind will expand, race forward, energized by our positive thoughts. Our visions allow us, for example, to be transformed from a member of the audience to the speaker on the stage. To see ourselves with that promotion we seek. All we need to do is be the speaker, be the promotion. If we begin to live the promotion we want, others will notice the growth and attitude we are radiating. Eventually, we obtain the promotion with our current employer, or seek another avenue to reach our goal. Our visions, when acted upon, create the leaps in our lives. They are more powerful than our knowledge. They open the door, and merely ask us to walk through. As Albert Einstein said, "Imagination is more important than knowledge."

The same dynamics are at play in a negotiation—in any interaction. We can approach a negotiation with a variety of biases. Biases create walls built by our egotude. For example, we may feel the other side is somehow "lesser" than we are, has already indicated its inability or unwillingness to be reasonable, or has trespassed upon us with earlier perceived insults. Perhaps the other side demanded the meeting be at a particular place (their office), a particular hour (inconvenient), or that particular participants be present (ones we wish weren't going to be in attendance). If we treat these demands as trespasses and bruises to our ego, we become invested in those biases and it becomes more difficult to listen to the other side. We lose the opportunity to gain their trust. Without their trust, it is more difficult to ask probing questions and hit pay dirt—strike oil. How will we understand the other side's wants and needs, the predicates upon which to build a solution?

Our simple everyday thoughts can either be negative or positive. Which switch will you flick prior to your next interaction? What tone will you set? Will it be a tone of disdain, or one that facilitates a relationship leading to trust and understanding? Of course, there will be circumstances where an acceptable solution may not be available.

For example, the police officer who stopped us may be working a holiday shift due to lack of seniority; his holiday is spoiled. Perhaps he even quarreled with his wife because he couldn't attend the family's holiday picnic. Who knows what baggage the police officer may be carrying to your encounter? You sense the officer is in a bad mood, not to be reckoned with. However, by putting aside your biases and burying your egotude, if nothing else you ought to be able to contain the situation. In so doing, you will most likely enable the officer to issue the least painful ticket possible. On the other hand, if we become argumentative or "flash our egotude," the officer will probably ticket us for the most serious violation possible.

If we address the situation without ego, then we can allow ourselves to accept that we were the one he caught, the one every other driver stares at as they speed by, grateful it wasn't them. It could have been another motorist, but instead it was you or me. Tough luck! Accept that reality. Instead of formulating your defense—which always reeks of attitude—accept the reality and you will most likely give off an aroma of respect, the recognition that the officer is simply doing his job. It may not help (although it usually will), but it surely won't hurt. You will have opened the door for the officer to respond in kind with a summons for a lesser offense.

Likewise, as we approach a scheduled negotiation with individuals with whom we have not been able to establish a rapport, we have two choices. On one hand, we can think positively and endeavor to build a bridge regardless of the reasons for the lack thereof so far. Ironically, the very act of positive thinking puts us in a position to overcome the negativities even if we really don't know why they exist. On the other hand, once we allow our biases and egotude to overcome us, we find ourselves short-circuiting our ability to create a rapport.

Positive thinking, which has been espoused and spoken about by so many, from Thoreau to Graham, can be practiced in the simplest of ways in the everyday encounters of life. It's not about working toward the Nobel Peace Prize. It's about our everyday interactions. Are you approaching each encounter with a positive attitude, or are you approaching too many encounters with bias and egotude? If the latter, it will imprison you in your own thoughts, and prevent you from seeing the other side's position. It will prevent you from working to find a solution.

When we think positively, we emit a positive vibration. When we think in terms of how we can help to solve the problem—whether it's a colleague who seeks our advice, or tension that developed by virtue of an unpleasant encounter between us and another—we find ourselves automatically exuding positive vibrations. Vibrations of goodness and kindness bubbling up from our self-replenishing reservoir of grace. By thinking positively, as a problem-solver, we begin to see issues and problems in ways that will tempt us to find solutions.

Positive thinking can be exhibited by sincerity. Imagine this situation. Your initial encounter with an adversary was strained and chilly. You walk into the meeting and:

- Sit down on your side of the table. You do not make eye contact.

  or

- You say, "You know, I think we got started on the wrong foot. Maybe, it was my fault because you caught me at a difficult moment during our first telephone conversation."

Which opening gambit do you think will move the meeting in a positive direction? Which response are you more likely to receive:

- An icy glare.

  or

- "Let's put our differences behind us and find a way to bridge them. I certainly want to."

Positive thinking unlocks us from our prison of Right. It allows us to recognize there may be many ways to be right. Often, to reach resolution, a compromise between several rights may be necessary. Once we become a positive thinker, our thought processes grow, and instead of overanalyzing each issue, some of which are minor, we begin to see the big picture. We don't feel the need to win every battle in the trenches of secondary or tertiary issues. Once we begin thinking globally, we will be able to better free-think the issues and see deeper into the other side's true needs, wants, and desires.

LISTENING!

Positive thinking fosters moments of epiphany, when a new idea comes to us. One we had not thought of before or that, at first blush, seemed so radical or unrealistic that we dismissed it. It may occur while we are thinking about a problem, perhaps while driving, or as we daydream watching television, or in our sleep. Although many greater thinkers have written and spoken about the epiphanies that occur while dreaming, embarrassment may nonetheless prevent us from writing them down and remembering them. They seem so out of the box, we are fearful that our colleagues, employer, or adversaries will deride us if we suggest the idea. Yet, more often than not, it may be that these thoughts—the ones that bubble up from our subconscious during our dreams—present the best paths to solving a problem. Sometimes they offer a new path in our lives. All too often, we refuse to "listen" to these thoughts, much less act upon them. We refuse to emancipate ourselves. Our fear of derision and scorn keeps us inside our "lock-less" prisons. Our jailers are fear of rejection and fear of failure.

If we think positively, however, we won't discard new ideas. Our positive thoughts will allow us to trust ourselves enough to share new ideas with ourselves—think them through—and then share them with others. Trust your instincts. Take a chance and trust yourself. Positive thoughts will promote positive actions. Trust your instincts. Oh, to be young again, we think, when instinct ruled. Well, it still does, but as we grow older, our instincts are often smothered by our fear of failure and rejection. Cast those fears aside. Walk out of your unlocked prison. Every moment of our lives is the threshold between the prison of our past and the freedom of our future.

Let's consider a classic scenario where rational thought often overrides the instinctual, all to our detriment. When two people first meet on a blind date they are, at that moment, best able to "feel" their natural instincts. To feel whether they will work as a couple. To feel how they fit. On a first date, neither party is invested in the relationship. This first encounter (and perhaps the next encounter as well) may be the only time the couple can allow themselves to truly feel their unadulterated instinctual emotions. They can really listen to what the other person has to say, and absorb their entire presence—emotional, spiritual, physical, and verbal.

However, once the parties proceed into the relationship and become intimate, neither can continue to be truly instinctual. Why? Because they have then become invested in the relationship. "Let's try to make it work" insinuates itself into each person's thinking. At this watershed in the relationship, when one or both say (or think), "Let's make it work since we've already gone this far," the parties no longer think instinctually. Rationalization infuses their thoughts. If the couple doesn't really mesh, one or both of them starts to say, "Even though X does so and so, I really want to give the relationship more of a chance. X will change" (Oh, how the divorce courts are filled with those who said, "I thought I could change him/her!"). They should have listened to the comedian, Flip Wilson, whose signature line was, "What you see is what you get!" In fact, what you see is what you get, for the most part, in life. Do those words put Flip Wilson in the same league as Thoreau? Hmmm. Mr. Wilson was simply saying that people seldom change.

It is painful to really look at ourselves and recognize our flaws. It is even harder (and rarer) to commit to change and follow through on it. Mr. Wilson was perhaps advising that each of us needs to allow ourselves to see the other person exactly for who and what they are. Why? Because that is most likely who, and what, we are almost always going to get. Yet, even when we sense a romantic relationship really isn't right, our investment in the relationship causes us to rationalize. The investment causes us to rationalize away our concerns by attempting to neutralize—attempting to smother—our instincts. This is a time to listen to your heart. Trust your instincts.

We tend to rationalize away our instincts too often in our everyday encounters as well, encounters of lesser significance than our love life. We must allow ourselves to free-think the deal—to free-think the relationship—no matter how difficult or painful. It's easy in a negotiation. The investment of time in a negotiation pales in significance to an investment of time and emotion in our love life. We seldom have to concern ourselves about the feelings of the other party to a negotiation if the deal dies. No matter what, it's just another deal. Do not emotionalize the deal. Use your power of positive thought to process issues and solve problems.

We can also actualize the concept of positive thinking through visualization. Simply visualize the smile and the yes we seek from the other side. By the same token, we can visualize ourselves saying yes and wearing a smile on our face. Radiate positivity. It will shine on the negotiation and enhance your ability to reach a solution. Start with a simple visualization of yes. Then visualize a completed deal or successful encounter. See it in the way you would like it to resolve. Visualize a successful ending to the play taking place on the stage in your mind. Visualize the police officer simply giving you a warning. See Gerhardt giving you the time slot you want. See the return clerk waiting on you and giving you a store credit or cash refund in exchange for your shirt, rather than making you return after her lunch break. By visualizing a successful ending, we automatically give off vibrations and aromas that will induce, perhaps even intoxicate (with our kindness) the other side to reach for a yes.

Many years ago, when I refocused my legal career to concentrate more on real estate than corporate law, I sought to find an industry organization in which to participate. Finally, after attending several conferences, I found an organization in which I felt comfortable. As I attended this particular organization's conferences, I was always impressed by the quality of its volunteer speakers. Then, one day, at one of their conferences, I visualized myself at the lectern giving a presentation. With that positive thought and visualization, I developed the confidence, even though I was relatively new to the industry, to seek a speaker's role at the next conference. It took a while to break in. Eventually, after volunteering for any speaker role regardless of importance, I was given a chance to speak. That opportunity was the springboard for my career in real estate. Years later, I became the chairman of the conference. The power of positive thought and visualization was much stronger than I could have possibly realized back then.

Sometimes, a positive thought or visualization is induced by another. Don't be so quick to disregard it or consider it an insincere compliment. Absorb all positivity coming in your direction. Assume sincerity! When I was a freshman at college, my father took me to buy a suit at his clothing store. I don't know why, but rather than helping me himself he asked his partner, Fred Wind, to help me. I finally found a suit to my liking, selected it, tried it on in the dressing room and walked back into the sales area to show my father and his partner. It was a dark blue suit with a dark blue matching vest. After looking at myself approvingly in the mirror, I turned and saw a great big smile on the face of Mr. Wind. He was a very aristocratic New Yorker of German descent, quite intimidating to me, and I don't recall ever seeing him smile before.

I still remember his words. More as an order than a wish, he said: "You'll wear this suit when you are inducted into the Phi Beta Kappa Honor Society." He believed I could do it, so I began to believe as well. I took his words at face value. Four years later, I wore that suit when I was awarded my Phi Beta Kappa key.

Do you find it difficult to see the big picture? Bias and egotude focus on each and every tree—or trespass—making it impossible to see the forest, or over the treetops to the mountain beyond. Perhaps it's not much more than an easily scalable hill! If we can't grasp the forest, how will we see the jugular issues, the key issues that, once resolved, will place the transaction firmly on the road to successful completion? By allowing ourselves to think positively, we can truly free-think a deal and see the big picture. The concept is not trite. What is trite is how often we remain entangled in the underbrush of egotude, focused on secondary or tertiary issues (perhaps where a trespass from a hurt occurred). How will we ever see to the next mountain?

Moments of epiphany present themselves in many ways, often

deceptive. They seldom, if ever, present themselves as a fully integrated thought or concept. Rather, they appear as bits and pieces of an idea or a concept. But those bits and pieces can be expanded upon and connected just like answers in a crossword puzzle. Simply continue to reflect on the idea or concept. Don't disregard it! Oftentimes, we dismiss our best ideas, whether they came to us via daydream, night dream, or otherwise. We do so simply because we remember them as incomplete or too risky, even seemingly outrageous. We reject them as we reflect in the harsh reality of a rational (perhaps morning) moment, failing to understand that the universe will give us the complete answer if we continue to focus on the pieces that were already delivered. Seldom will the universe give us the heavens and the earth in one fell swoop. Remember, it took six days to create the world—it didn't happen overnight, nor was Rome built in a day (Rome, Italy, that is).

We can all become better negotiators and more effective and fulfilled individuals if we allow ourselves to exhibit more of the grace of kindness, goodness, and understanding. We simply need the right attitude—the one that allows us to think positively. If you are wearing shoes of bad attitude, change them. They're unattractive, and they pinch. You always feel better if your feet feel good. Am I right? Change to those comfortable, attractive shoes of positive attitude. It's really that easy. You are in sole command of the attitude you are wearing.

We truly are what we think. Persistent thoughts, positive or negative, will first become words and then turn into actions. So why not be positive? It's as easy as turning on the positive switch. Like a light switch, if it was turned off (and it doesn't matter who turned it off, or when, or even why), just turn it back on. Don't let anybody turn your switch off. Wear those "smile shoes." Be the honest and kind person that you are and slip on those shoes of grace.

Life is a series of choices. We can reflect upon the trespasses of the past, and look to get even or otherwise justify our anger. But if we do, we continue to live in the past. How can we go forward if we are expending our energy looking back? Even worse, if we are wasting energy on negative pursuits.

How often have you found yourself reflecting on a past insult stemming from an interaction with a co-worker or friend? Perhaps, at the time, it just passed over your head, yet that night you remained awake, restless as you seethed over what you now felt was a piercing verbal jab. We've all been subjected to these hurts, and we've all rethought the interchange and what we would have wanted to say if the relationship permitted (the jab may have been spoken by a superior), or we were quicker-witted. Your ego scores these types of encounters as defeats. But why? You weren't defeated! You were simply caught off-guard by someone who either delivered an unintentional hurt, or had to massage his own insecurity by allowing his egotude to surface with a mean-spirited comment.

If you let the trespass roll off your back, you win.

If you let those feelings fester and mentally replay the incident until you've re-enacted it the way you wished it had occurred, you lose.

Some call this reflection ruminating, but that does not adequately describe the pain, and damage, we inflict upon ourselves by revising the reality to assuage our ego. We are falsifying reality to get even mentally, allowing ourselves to see the with the anger of the hurt, and we enflame that anger with our exploding egotude. How has this process of rumination helped you? It hasn't. If the process started before you went to bed, it probably delayed your falling asleep. If the process started during the day, it probably caused you to lose your focus on whatever task was at hand. This mental rescripting of an unpleasant interaction is always for naught. There is no do-over for hurts, just foolish overreactions. If you wish to think positively and exhibit a positive mental attitude, remove rumination from your life. Don't confuse positive thinking with any type of get-even thinking. Get-even thinking is poison no matter what the name—reflection, rumination, or revenge.

Success in life is as simple as putting one foot in front of the other and moving confidently in the direction of your goal. You will reach

LISTENING!

your goal line. Then you'll visualize new goal lines. Simply avoid the defense's tacklers by using grace, kindness, and understanding. Ignore the inevitable trespasses. They might tackle us for one play, but they cannot stop us from getting up to be in the next play.

Why not assume people can read your negative thoughts, at least the ones about them.

PRACTICE POINTS

- We are what and how we think.

- Think "I can, I will," not "I'll try, I'll see."

- Remove "I'll try" from your thought process.

- Think of your thoughts as the clothing you are wearing. As if everyone can see them. Sometimes they can.

- Always move forward confidently in the direction of your goals. Only you can stop yourself from achieving them.

CONCLUSION

LISTENING!

E very negotiation constitutes a constantly changing mosaic of human emotions, relevant facts, and germane issues, all of which blend together. They are then often intertwined with a host of outside factors ranging from airplane schedules to personal issues such as family illness or family celebrations. A negotiation is a microcosm of life.

A skilled negotiator is able to deal effectively with all the elements of life. The skilled negotiator understands the factual predicates and legal and business issues. Equally important, he understands the human element that constitutes the drama of the negotiation. There are those who might say a degree in psychology is almost as important as a degree in law or business. Whatever the education, it should be coupled with the advisor's knowledge of the client's particular business. A skilled negotiator is an actor, advisor, director, lawyer, and psychologist all at once. Depending on the nature of the client's business, the skilled negotiator may be called upon to be an engineer, economist, architect, scientist, or other specialist. Use grace and positivity, and prepare fully; then, you will succeed whatever the outcome.

PS: Having just finished reading this book, you have already become a better negotiator. Why? By having read and reflected on what you have read, you have enhanced your negotiating skills. Now, read this book again. Why not? There's stuff you glossed over, perhaps stuff you didn't fully internalize. There's no extra charge. Why not give it a second pass? Go back to Chapter 1 . . . I'll be waiting.

PPS: The Skill of Reading—Many of the techniques we have discussed apply equally to becoming a better, more effective reader. How often do we skim passages we think we already understand, or which are seemingly irrelevant to us, or appear repetitive? How often do we read passages without really reading them, because we are distracted by other thoughts—a problem at the office or at home, or plans for the weekend or a long-awaited vacation?

Were you distracted from time to time? Did you catch yourself and reread the passages you skimmed? Was it worth the bother? Did you accept the key themes in the book, or reject them as obvious, lofty, or unrealistic? If you rejected them, why did you? Did the concept of working to become a kinder, gentler, more graceful person seem too "soft" in our hard-driving, work-oriented society? Do you think embracing those concepts will make you a less effective negotiator? Perhaps make you look weak to your colleagues or adversaries?

To the contrary, you will be seen as stronger. In fact, you will become stronger. How do I know? I know because, as a young lawyer, I exhibited many of the foibles I am urging you to shed. I needed, so I thought, to always try to be the sharpest knife in the room, the smartest person in the meeting. Why? Because my insecurities pushed me to constantly prove to others how smart I was. I sat in meetings "chomping at the bit" to speak, even if I sometimes cut another off. I leaped at every chance to make what I thought were my smarter, more incisive comments.

That was then. Over the years, I have learned the techniques I discuss in this book. I am still just as smart and incisive as I was before. However, I am much more experienced. Now, experienced enough to know that these techniques and concepts really work. Now, if I make mistakes, I seek to immediately fix them, regardless of my perceived embarrassment in the admission and corrective action. Now, if I offend another, I apologize. I apologize to their face, flat out.

I wrote this second postscript to reinforce my belief that the material in this book will enhance all of your negotiating and other interpersonal

LISTENING!

skills. It may well help your walk down the path of becoming a kinder, gentler, more graceful being—a path we all strive to walk.

I loved writing this book. Thank you for reading it. I have written two other books, *Leading* and *Launching*, completing a trilogy which I hope will enhance your business endeavors and personal encounters. If you are interested in purchasing the books, please visit www.amazon.com. I would love your comments and feedback, so please feel free to email me at jnewman@sillscummis.com.

NOTES

LISTENING!

LISTENING!

LISTENING!

www.ingramcontent.com/pod-product-compliance
Lightning Source LLC
Chambersburg PA
CBHW061944070426
42450CB00007BA/1048